For you. Always you.

NIGHT XPOSED

Dear Fantasy Girl...

An exquisite collection of erotica stories

Published in 2009 by Lulu

Lulu Enterprises Inc.

3101 Hillsborough Street, Raleigh, NC 27607

Visit:

http://stores.lulu.com/nightxposed

http://www.myspace.com/nightxposed

ISBN: 978-0-578-01038-0

Printed in the United States of America

Author's Note

No one is more surprised than I that I am writing this note right now. I never dreamed that what started as a simple 1,000 word throw-away story entered in a writing contest on MySpace could turn into this. As a writer, erotica was never my chosen genre. It just kind of happened.

After the surprising response I received in the contest, I thought it might be fun to create a blog where I could post a few of the stories that were floating around in my head, so I created the Night Xposed page on MySpace. Its reception by readers was overwhelming. There are approximately 300,000 blogs posted on MySpace every day and by the third Night Xposed blog, they were consistently in the top 10 in the blog rankings. Within two months time, every new blog posted on that page went to #1, thanks to a wonderful group of dedicated and loyal readers. Who'da thunk? Not me.

To make a long story short, with the success of the page, I was approached about publishing a collection of the blogs and you are holding the result in your hand.

Included in this collection are eleven of the blogs that were originally posted on the Night Xposed page. The remaining stories are new and can only be found here. I hope you enjoy them.

Join me at **www.myspace.com/nightxposed**

Foreword

Erotica is like silk and velvet, it's about touch and taste, it's pure pleasure and temptation... An erotica writer gives you the choice of opening your mind, allowing your deepest desires to fully manifest themselves.

Night Xposed is a name that is synonymous with fine erotica. An exceptionally talented writer, Night Xposed is capable of taking the reader on a delightful intimate journey right from the first paragraph. Every story is a long, sensual ride that flows brilliantly, touching all of your senses, firing your imagination. With daring, vivid descriptions, the storylines will capture the attention of anyone who is ready to explore not only the beauty of the human body but also the intense passion translated into lust and love.

Night Xposed's stories will engage the mind as well as the body with each of the unforgettable experiences of the man who forever seeks his fantasy girl. She is always there, inspiring and perfect, just like a sensual muse. Every woman recognizes her own desires in fantasy girl, while every man is longing to touch her beauty in more ways than one.

An exquisite selection of erotica stories, *"Dear Fantasy Girl..."* a Night Xposed collection, is a must have for anyone who wants to discover the physical and emotional expressions of passion and devotion toward a beloved one...

LMC

Table of Contents

HOW CAN I TELL HER?

© Bjorn Oldsen

How can I tell her how I feel?

How can I tell her that her face is ever present in my mind's eye? That is where I seek her and her beauty overwhelms me. I sit and stare at her for hours and cannot look away. I suddenly gasp and draw a deep breath and realize that I've forgotten to breathe. I'll notice that my heart is racing and I feel the flush in my face. And then I stare at her again.

How can I tell her that I want to breathe her in and never exhale again? I long to know her scent and to smell her on my clothing long after she is gone. I need to breathe in her sweet breath moments before I taste it for the first time. Just one breath and her aroma will be so familiar that every other scent will pale against her fragrance.

How can I tell her that she consumes me? The fire in my soul yearns to burst forth from my lips and from my fingertips to enflame her passion. She burns so brightly for me that the mere touch of her fingers would scorch my flesh and leave me in ashes, to be scattered at the will of her breath.

How can I tell her that my lips exist only to find hers? The anticipation of true love's first kiss haunts my dreams, the first touch of tongue waiting impatiently in fantasy. They seek her in dream and in caprice and when they find her there, they drink deeply. These same lips that may utter nary a sound but to speak her name.

How can I tell her that it is more than my arms that are empty without her? The softness of her body held close, the fullness of her breast pressed to mine, the merging of spirit with the merging of flesh, the sweetness of her touch at the back of my neck, the ecstasy of my fingers through her hair, every movement forming the chimera of my existence.

How can I tell her the depth of my desire? Our bodies entwined so tightly, I cannot tell where hers ends and mine begins. The touch of her velvet hand as she guides me to her, beseeching warm acquiescence and finding blessed penetration of body and soul. The gentle motion beneath me, the most caring stroke above me, the tender embrace enfolding me and the sweet release of essence as one.

How can I tell her of the swelling of lust that overcomes me? Raw, unbridled obsession igniting passion's flame, burning to the breadth and depth of my soul. Desperate need surpassing want, intense heat overtaking warmth, teeth leave their mark, nails blaze a path, the furious piercing of engorged flesh by enraged longing, savagely driving to fierce crescendo and violent, convulsing eruption. And in the quiet moments after contented collapse, I will love her.

How can I find the words to make her come to me? I have nothing to offer her but would give her everything. She is destined to step from my fantasies. And when she does, what will I say to her? I know not the words, except for these...

I love you twice as much as I did yesterday. And yesterday, I loved you so very much.

COME BACK TO ME

Hello, fantasy girl. How can I be missing you so much when I've never touched you, never held you, never seen you move? You exist only in my mind, yet I am missing you to the point of physical pain.

I miss the beauty and grace of your face. A face to rival any classic beauty...a face that could only have been created by the hand of God. I am so in awe of how amazingly beautiful you are. No matter how many times I look at you, my heart always beats faster. You take my breath each time. The incredible brightness of your eyes, the perfectly shaped eyebrows, the beautiful symmetry of your nose, the pure line of your jaw and chin, the lift of your cheeks when you smile, and your perfect, perfect lips, full, ripe and ready.

How I long to feel that first kiss with you, faces inches apart, drowning in the brilliant pools of your eyes, feeling the pounding of my heart as I move one hand to your cheek, pushing your hair back from your face and leaning forward to touch my lips to yours. Lingering there, lips pressing lightly together. Slipping my hand behind your neck, pulling you closer, lips now slightly parted and savoring the tingle that passes through our bodies as our tongues meet for the first time. As our passion builds, so does the urgency of our tongues, exploring each other's mouths, entwined together, pressed tightly, sucking your tongue into my mouth and never letting it go.

I miss your breasts, the breasts I've never seen. But I have seen them so many times in my mind's eye, so perfect, your nipples erect, my hands and mouth insatiable. I bury my face in them, rubbing my face over every inch of them. Taking your breasts into my hands and massaging, caressing, squeezing, rubbing back and forth over your nipples with my thumbs, feeling them rise. Moving my mouth to them and drawing circles around them with the tip of my tongue. Pulling them into my mouth and flicking them with my tongue, kneading them… needing them. Pulling at them with my lips, biting at them with my teeth, feeling them stiffen just as you make me stiffen. Feeling them wrapped around me.

I miss your legs, your long, perfectly formed legs… stretched out before me, standing in front of me, wrapped tightly around me. I miss your belly, your most beautiful and perfect belly. I miss your feet, your cute toes, the sweet curve of instep. I miss your hands…moving over my body, wrapping them around my desire, lightly stroking, thin fingers sliding over your own body, touching and penetrating as I watch.

I miss the sweet taste of your sex, my tongue exploring, flicking, teasing. I miss the pleasure of your perfect thighs pressed against each side of my face, parting your sweet lips with the tip of my tongue, circling your clit and enjoying the feeling of it beginning to swell. Running my tongue up and down each side of your engorged bud, tasting your pink flesh, breathing in your sweet scent, savoring the feel of wetness against lips, heat against tongue. Flicking my tongue rapidly and firmly against your tiny button, moving faster and faster until it is as tight and hard as a stone. Pulling it between my lips and sucking it hard while my tongue circles it inside my mouth. Slipping my tongue deep inside you as you press into me, fucking you hard with my tongue…pounding it in and out of your pussy. Sucking you into my mouth while my fingers seek out your entrance and plunge into you. My fingers pumping in and out of your hot, wet pussy while my lips pull at your clit. Feeling your pussy clenching tightly around my fingers as your climax starts to build. Feeling your entire body convulsing and hearing you scream as you cum violently, bucking against my face and gripping the back of my head tightly. Enjoying the feeling of knowing, as you collapse, completely sated, that I can give you as much pleasure as you have ever had.

I miss your mouth, lips and tongue…your lips nibbling at my cock, your tongue teasing up and down my shaft, taking me into your mouth, sucking on the tip while running your tongue over its head, taking me deep and fucking me, my entire body spasming as I explode deep into your throat.

I miss fucking you. I miss placing the head of my cock against your wet pussy and the feel of it sliding into you. Moving slowly in and out of you, trying to make it last as long as I can, slowly building your desire, your need. Feeling you respond and your hips rising up to meet me as my cock fills you. The feel of your pussy wrapped tightly around me as I slide slowly all the way out to the tip and slowly all the way back deep inside you. Watching your face, your eyes closed tightly as I begin to fuck you faster and harder. Feeling your hands on my ass, pulling me deeply into you, your hips rocking beneath me, fucking me fervently.

I miss grabbing you behind the neck and holding you down over the arm of the couch, my cock pumping in and out of you from behind, stretching your pussy tight. Fucking you hard and fast, our bodies sweaty and pulsating as I pound into you, your hips bouncing and your ass slamming back into me. My balls slapping against your fingers as you rub your clit furiously while I fuck you relentlessly. Fucking so hard, cock pounding in and out, pussy so hot and wet, clutching so tightly and cumming so hard that we collapse in a heap, unable to move.

I miss your incredible, perfect ass. I miss you on your knees, leaning on your forearms, your ass in the air. I can see my face buried in it, covering it with kisses. Tonguing you, making you wet and ready to be penetrated. Fucking your ass with my tongue, burying it deep inside you, plunging in, pulling out, plunging deeper. I can see myself kneeling behind you, my raging cock in my hand, placing the head against your puckered opening. Watching as your hands move to your cheeks and you spread your ass for me. Staring mesmerized as just the tip enters you and your tightness keeps me from going any farther. I press harder against you and hear you gasp as the head moves through your entrance. I watch, enamored, as you adjust to the thickness of my cock and begin to push back against me. I watch it slide slowly, deeper and deeper into you until it is completely buried in your ass.

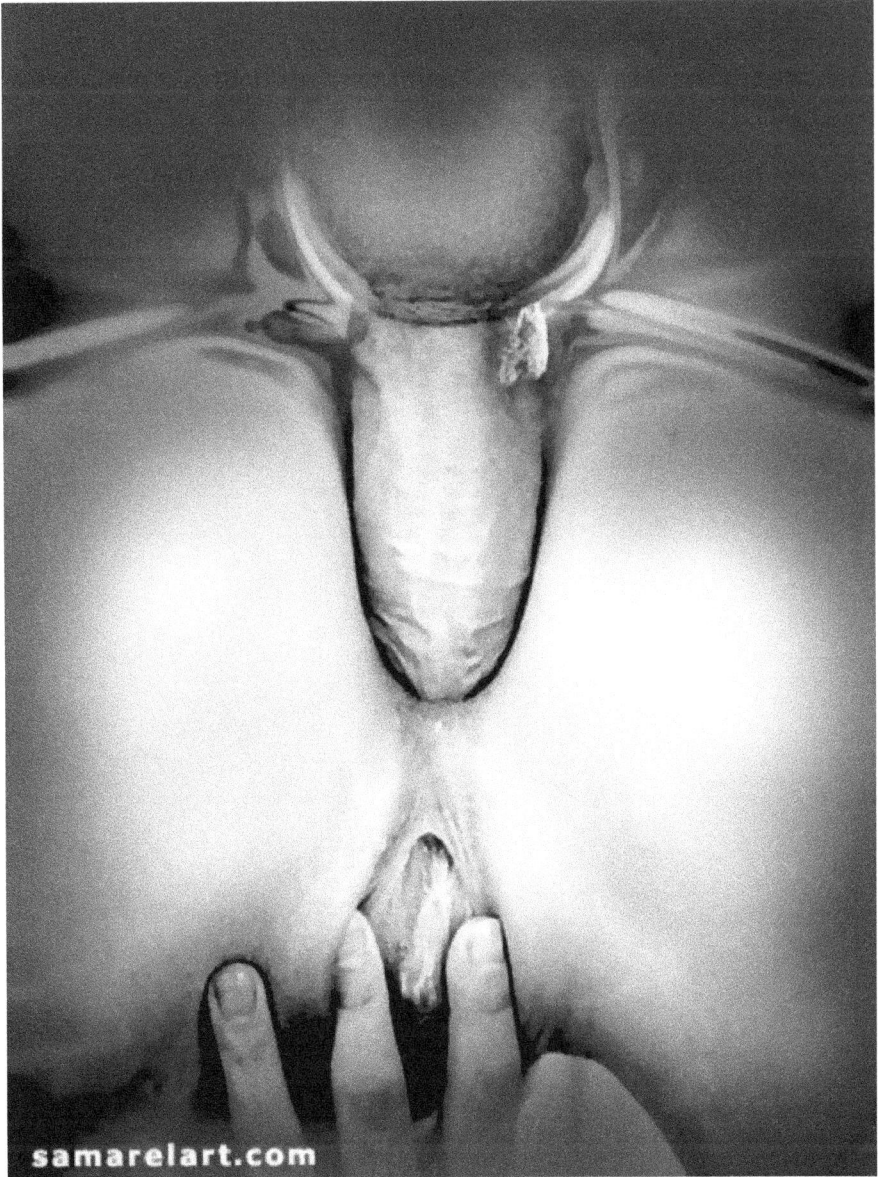

samarelart.com

I feel your finger move to your clit as I begin to move inside you. Your ass is gripping me so tightly, I know I will cum in just a stroke or two, but I can't wait and begin to pump in and out of you. Your finger works frantically at your clit and you moan with pleasure. My cock is splitting you in two, pounding into your ass and it is more pleasure than I can stand. Your fingers find their way into your pussy and you are rubbing desperately at your clit with your fingers, slamming your ass back into me, taking us over the top and together we cum, bodies jerking, hips rocking, legs shaking.

I don't know how I can miss all of these things that I've never had, but I do. Perhaps because I know you are real. I know you are out there somewhere. I know you are so much more than fantasy. I miss you terribly. One day, you will be mine.

IN MY DREAMS

Hello, fantasy girl. I dreamed of you again last night.

I know it had to be a dream, yet it felt so very real to me. I woke up in the middle of the night and there you were, in my doorway across the room. You were standing in shadow, but I knew it was you. I recognized the beautiful swell of your breast and the perfect curve of your hip. There was one stray moonbeam shining through the bedroom window, illuminating your hair and giving it a soft glow. I tried to reach out to you but for some reason, I couldn't move. You began to move slowly across the room. I watched you glide toward me as if you were floating, your feet not quite touching the floor. When you reached the side of the bed, you let your robe slide from your shoulders and fall to the floor and you stood naked before me. You stood there momentarily and let my eyes drink in the beauty of your naked body in the moonlight.

Just when my eyes were full to overflowing, you slowly climbed onto the bed and swung one leg over me so that you were above me, your hands at each of my shoulders and your knees at each of my hips. You lowered your face slowly towards mine, your hair hanging down around my face and tickling my cheeks. But the fall of your hair also kept your face in shadow and all I could make out was the radiance of your eyes. You paused, your lips an inch away from mine. I tried to reach up to meet you, but I still couldn't move. You hovered over me. I could smell jasmine in your hair and the sweetness of your breath. Then slowly and ever so softly, your lips touched mine. Your kiss was soft and sweet and gentle, your lips full and perfect. I parted my lips and felt the flick of your tongue against mine. Never have I experienced such a beautiful kiss. For several minutes, you kissed me so sensually. It was made all the more erotic by my inability to move and giving over complete control to you.

You slowly lowered your body closer to mine. Your breasts brushed against my chest. As we continued our kiss, I could feel your nipples begin to stiffen against my chest, just as I was beginning to stiffen against your thigh. I so wanted to move my hands to your breasts, to cup them, to circle my palms softly against your nipples, to brush them with the tips of my fingers, but I was still frozen, unable to move. You must have felt my desire, because you moved up and brought your breasts even with my face. You lowered one perfect breast to my mouth and I took your nipple softly between my lips, circling it gently with my tongue. It gave me such warmth to feel it swelling under the touch of my lips. After a few moments, you gave me the other breast and as I tasted it, a soft moan escaped your lips.

I begged you to slide your body further up so I could feel your perfect belly against my cheek, so I could cover every inch of your most beautiful belly with kisses before moving down to what I was really longing to taste, but you shook your head, your hair brushing my face. Instead, I felt your hand sliding slowly down my chest and over my stomach until your fingers were lightly tickling my pubic hair. Your lips returned to mine and our tongues gently circled each other. You continued to tease me, your fingers so near the base of my member, but not quite touching it, bringing me to a serious state of arousal. When I thought I could not stand it any longer, you took my cock into your hand. The warmth of your hand enveloping me was like fire and I don't think I have ever been so hard. You stroke me slowly and softly, your hand moving tenderly from the base of the shaft all the way up over its head and then slowly back down again. Over and over, your hand moved up and down my cock, sometimes pausing at its peak to rub your thumb gently over the head before continuing your soft and slow strokes.

My breath began to quicken and you must have known that I would not last much longer under the touch of your velvet hand. You shifted and positioned yourself directly over my engorged cock. You lowered your hips and with your hand still wrapped around me, you began rubbing the head of my cock against your clit. Back and forth over your clit, slowly at first but then a bit faster, a bit more urgently. I could feel your button swelling against the head of my cock as you rubbed them together. It was so incredibly erotic! Your breathing began to get heavier. Now, you were moving me faster and faster against you and increased the strokes to include the entire length of your pussy. From clit to opening and back again, over and over. The very tip of my cock would just barely penetrate your sweetest of openings before you would slide it back to rub it against your swollen clit again. You were so wet and so warm against me. Your breath was hot against my neck and your nipples, firm against my chest. I begged you to end this torture. You placed the head of my cock against the hot, wet opening of your pussy and began to slide down over me. Just as the head of my cock slid into your tight, wet pussy...

I woke up!!!!

It was so frustrating! I closed my eyes and tried to return to you, desperately needing to fall back to sleep, but it was no use. I was so hard for you! Although I could not return to my dream of you, I could still close my eyes and see you there before me in the moonlight. So I closed my eyes, wishing that it was your hand on me instead of my own. And before long, it WAS your hand stroking me softly. It was your tongue teasing the shaft of my cock and circling its head. It was your velvet hand guiding me deep inside you. It was your sweet pussy clenching tightly around my cock. And just as you always do, you made me cum so hard.

MASS TRANSIT

I see you for the first time and I have to pause to catch my breath. You are a vision of beauty, of sexuality, of confidence. Everything that I knew you would be. I stand and watch for a moment as you move up the street, completely hypnotized by your walk, your perfect ass, your finely sculpted legs, the curve of your hip, your flawless back and the beautiful, glowing hair that drapes it. I turn to follow you and when you get on the bus at 8th Avenue, I do the same. Every eye on the bus watches you as you move up the aisle. I smile as I watch each man you pass pull in his stomach and puff out his chest before I realize that I'm doing the same thing. After a few stops, you step off the bus and I follow you as you head toward the train, evidently heading for the city. As I follow, my mind wanders, imagining the two of us together in the city and I smile at the thought. I follow you onto the subway, enjoying the sway of your ass as you move.

The train is crowded this morning. Several men rise to offer their seat, but you say no thank you and grab a pole at the rear of the car. As I move through the crowd toward you, our eyes meet. I expect you to look away, but you don't and our eyes remain locked until I pass by and step up close behind you. The train moves with a jolt and I stumble slightly and bump up against you. I apologize and you look back at me over your shoulder, but say nothing, your face expressionless. But your eyes linger, locked on mine for just a moment.

At the Atlantic Avenue station, more people push their way onto the already crowded train and I find myself jostled closer to you until your shoulders are against my chest. I expect you to move away from me, but we are packed in tight and there is nowhere for you to go. As the train begins to move again, I reach out and take hold of the pole to steady myself and our hands touch. You don't move yours away. I close my eyes and breathe in the scent of your hair. Your smell is sweet and intoxicating and the feel of your back against my chest and that oh so slight touch of my hand against yours begins to excite me and I can feel my cock beginning to swell in my pants.

A curve in the track causes you to sway back against me and the slope of your ass fits perfectly into the cavity at the top of my thighs. I feel embarrassment that you must be able to feel my growing cock in the small of your back, but if you do, you make no sign, nor do you move away. Perhaps you can't, but perhaps you don't want to. The motion of the train causes you to sway back and forth against my cock and I find myself bending my knees slightly to bring it from the small of your back down to your ass. To my surprise, you rise up taller and my cock is now firmly against the crack of your ass. You begin to move your ass side to side, up and down, grinding it against my now raging cock. Faces of strangers are inches away from ours and I look to see if anyone is recognizing what is happening, but see no evidence of it. As you move against me, I feel that familiar tightening in my balls and pit of my stomach and I begin to push harder against you, moving my ass back and forth as if we were fucking. Again to my surprise, I feel a hand on my cock, rubbing it hard and fast through my pants. It gives me courage and I reach my free hand under your skirt and am pleasantly surprised to find you are not wearing panties. I rub my fingers over your clit and slide a finger inside you. You are already moist and ready. I feel your hand taking down my fly and you reach inside my pants and release my cock. The risk of being found out has my cock as hard as it has ever been. I bend my knees further to bring myself in line with you and I feel you arching your back and pushing your ass out further into me. Your hand guides my cock against your wet opening and you rub its head against your slit until it finally slides inside you, giving me one of the greatest moments of excitement and pleasure I've ever had.

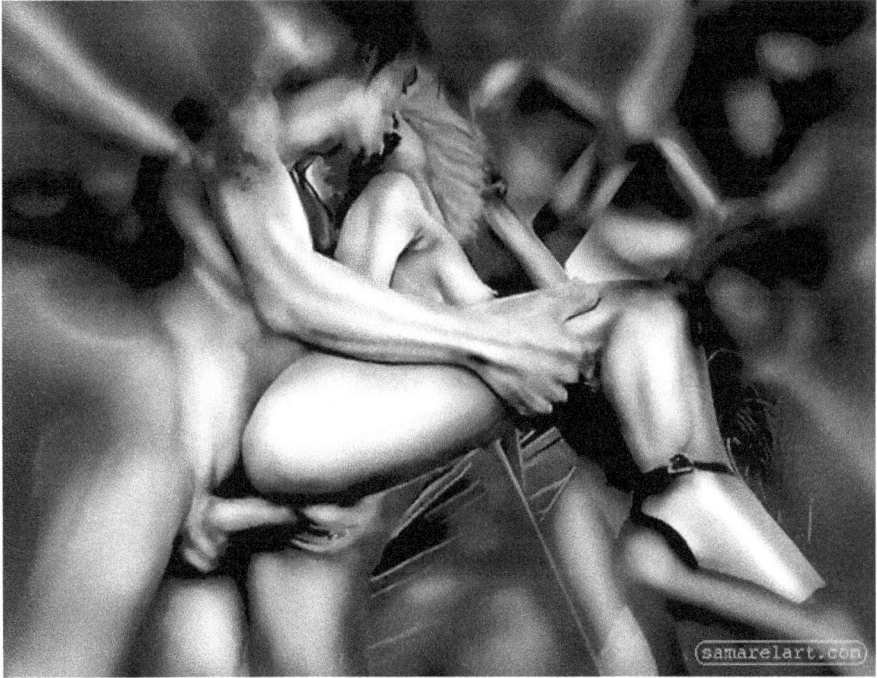

People are pressed tight against us on all sides, but we are oblivious as my cock moves in and out of you with the movement of the train. You are grinding back against me and I am pressing as tightly into you as I possibly can. We barely have to move as the motion of the train moves my cock inside you all on its own. I look to the right and the woman standing there against us is staring straight into my eyes. Her body is tight against the side of my leg, her crotch at my hip. There is a moist film over her eyes and I can feel her hand moving frantically against my hip. We are squeezed too tightly together for me to look down but I know that her fingers are pushing hard against her clit. The man in the suit pressed against your left side is breathing heavy and his face is flushed.

My cock continues to move inside you but I can feel my orgasm building and know I will not last more than a few more strokes. Suddenly, you grip the pole with both hands and I can feel you start to shudder and know that you are starting your climax. You throw your head back and I can feel your juices sliding down my cock as it moves in and out of you. I close my eyes, take a sharp breath and explode inside you in the most intense orgasm I have ever experienced. Your pussy pulses tightly around my cock as you continue to cum, bringing me a flood of orgasmic pleasure. My knees weaken and I can no longer stand. If we were not packed in so tightly, I would collapse to the floor, but I am held tightly in place by those around us.

The train arrives at Grand Street, the doors open and people begin to pile out, with my cock still buried inside you. Quickly, I pull out of you and tuck my spent member back into my pants. Your skirt drops back down into place. Several people are looking at us, strange looks on their face. The man in the suit steps away and tries to cover the stain on his pants with his briefcase. The woman to the right gives us a sheepish grin, her face flushed and covered with a thin layer of moisture. As she exits the train, she looks back over her shoulder and gives us a wink.

You turn to me and say "Hello, stranger...I was hoping to see you this morning." I respond, "Hello, fantasy girl," and take your hand in mine.

COME TO VEGAS

© Steve Anderson Photography

I'm sending you a plane ticket for Las Vegas and of course, some cash for the tables. When you arrive at the airport, take a cab to Caesar's Palace and go to the VIP line at the registration desk. I've added you to my account, so just give them your name. Check in…they already have my credit card so you won't need anything except your ID. Your room is on the 29th floor of the Palace Tower. Go up and unpack …get comfortable…get settled in.

You will find a bottle of champagne on ice and a large vase of gardenias on the marble bar next to the armoire. Immerse your face in the flowers and breathe deeply. Now pour yourself a glass of champagne and take it into the bathroom.

You will find a bottle of bubble bath next to the tub…pour yourself a hot bath, with plenty of bubbles. Climb in with your champagne, lie back and let the hot water envelop your body. If you like, you can turn on the water jets, but don't use them for anything except relaxation…I need you to save *that* for later. Close your eyes and savor the heat of the water against your skin, the cool of the champagne against your tongue and the scent of bubble bath filling the steamy air.

When the water begins to cool, step out and dry yourself slowly with the thick, fluffy cotton towels left for you by the side of the tub. When you are ready, stand in front of the full length mirror in the bedroom and dress yourself. I want everyone to marvel at your perfection as you move through the hotel.

Wear your shortest skirt to highlight your perfectly formed legs, bare from just below your bottom at your ankles. Wear your tiniest little, low-cut blouse, exposing your superbly flawless belly and accentuating your outstanding breasts. Show off your beautiful feet, your toes, the curve of your instep, your thin, perfect ankles…wear something strappy with a four inch heel. Leave your hair down, framing your breathtaking face. Now stand before the mirror and admire your beauty, knowing you are the most incredibly exquisite woman that has ever stood before it. It's time for Vegas to experience you.

Take the elevator down to the casino level and when you exit the elevator, follow the signs to the main entrance on the Strip. Feel every eye on you as you move through the casino…smile as dealers stop dealing to watch you pass by…enjoy as every head turns as you pass. Work it as only you can…every man you pass, look him straight in the eye, toss your hair back and smile…give him your sexiest walk as he turns to follow you with his eyes.

Just before you get to the main entrance, you will see a raised platform to your right with gaming tables. Go up the four steps and walk to the second roulette wheel on your right. Stand there for a moment to let the dealer and the other players drink you in, then step up to the table and buy $500 in $25 chips. Bet any three numbers you like and 26 for me. After your number hits, collect your winnings and continue to play. Enjoy yourself, get to know your fellow players, show them your wit, flirt with them, tease them, drive them out of their minds.

You look around and see me across the room, sitting at a blackjack table watching you. Our eyes meet and linger on each other for just a moment. You turn back to the table, slightly flushed, oddly excited, feeling my eyes on your back, feeling them burn from your ankles, up over your calves, your thighs, the small of your back. Knowing exactly what you are doing, you place a bet on the number furthest from you, causing you to lean far over the table. You stretch just a bit further than you really need to, linger there a bit longer than you really need to, knowing that your skirt is climbing up, showing me the briefest glimpse of your perfect ass in your thong. Unable to resist, you glance back over your shoulder to make sure you are getting the desired effect, but I'm not there. You frown slightly and turn back to the spinning wheel. You continue to play, occasionally glancing around the room, seeing every eye on you, except for mine.

A crowd has gathered around the table, drawn by the unrelenting need to be near you, to feast on you with their eyes, to be near enough to breathe in your beauty. You feel burning eyes again, you breathe in sharply and your heart rate quickens, but you don't turn around. The dealer says, "Place your bets" and spins the wheel. As seductively as you can (which is VERY seductively... unequaled by any other), you again lean far out over the table, up on your tiptoes, one foot raised up off the floor in your sexiest pose, the cheeks of your ass peeking out from beneath your skirt and fully exposing the delicious white triangle of cloth barely covering your sex. Again, you linger there, fully aware of the reaction you are causing. Only it isn't the burning eyes you feel this time. The briefest whisper of a touch starts behind your knee, moves up the back of your leg and trails off as it passes up over the curve of your ass. You gasp audibly and a shiver runs through your body. You don't even notice that your number hit until the dealer pushes the stack of chips in front of you.

Now you look back over your shoulder, but I'm no longer there. You turn back to the table and see me standing across the table, directly opposite you. Again, you can feel the heat rising in your cheeks and your breathing becomes heavy. Your eyes meet mine and you consider briefly playing coy with me, but you know I can see the hunger in your eyes. Several of the men you flirted with before I arrived attempt to talk to you, but you don't hear them, your eyes never leaving mine. In spite of the dinging of slot machines, the clanging of coins dropping into trays, the shouts of people as they win, or lose, for the two of us, there is total silence. It's as if we are the only two people in the room… everything moving in slow motion.

Never taking my eyes away from yours, I put cash down on the table and the dealer says "Welcome back, sir" and exchanges it for chips. He says, "Place your bets" once again and the moment is broken. We both begin to play as if nothing has happened, without exchanging another glance or uttering a single word. You return your attention to the crowd that has gathered around you and I feign concentration on the game. I am utterly captivated by your incredible beauty, seeing you live for the first time, and I never let you out of the corner of my eye.

After several spins, one of your numbers hits again and you ask the dealer to cash you out. As you pick up your winnings from the table, you pause and look directly into my eyes, heat clearly visible in them. Then you turn and walk away, followed by several of the men you have bewitched. I play a couple of more spins of the wheel and then ask to be cashed out as well.

You are sitting at the bar, surrounded by men that cannot pull themselves away from you. You juggle their attention with a skill that is unmatched. You feel me before you see me. As you sit there, you suddenly feel the light touch of a finger slipping past the waist of your skirt, under the band of your thong and sliding softly across your lower back at the top of your ass. Again, a shiver passes through your body and you feel the tingle in your sex and in your nipples. You turn and see me walking to the end of the bar and I can feel you watching me as I order a drink. When the bartender brings me my drink, I turn to face you and once again, our eyes lock.

I watch you as the man next to you leans in and says something to you in an effort to draw your attention. Your eyes break from mine and you turn to him. I can see from the expression on your face that you are not being very pleasant with him and I pick up my drink and walk toward you. He rises from his stool, a look of dejection on his face, and I slip into it before any of the many others surrounding you can do so. You turn to face me and hear my voice for the first time, "Hello, fantasy girl."

We sit facing each other, staring into each other's eyes, not saying a word. I would like to say that it is because I'm playing it cool, making you desire me with just my eyes. But the truth is, I'm made speechless by your breathtaking beauty. Your gorgeous eyes burn through me, the perfect symmetry of your nose, your full pink lips slightly parted, the remarkable angle of your chin, the exquisite cheekbones that make your beauty classic. But mostly, it is your eyes. Your big, beautiful, brilliant eyes. Seeing you before me, in the flesh, staggeringly beautiful, I can barely catch my breath. You are so much more stunning than I could ever have imagined you in my fantasies. Although it is my heart that is pounding, my cock can't help but respond as well and I feel it beginning to swell.

Gradually, the admirers around you wander off as they recognize they have lost any hope of your attention and we are left alone at the bar, eyes locked. We stare at each other without saying a word, enjoying our drinks, each seeing the want in the other's eyes. Occasionally, I place my hand on your back, slipping my pinkie inside the waistband of your skirt as my hand travels lightly across your bare lower back.

After long minutes of taking each other in, I reach down and place my hand on your thigh. You uncross your legs and spread them slightly, telling me everything I need to know. I move very close to you in an attempt at discretion and slowly slide my hand up your thigh until my thumb is resting at the top of your panty line and my index finger is resting directly against your sex. I can feel the moisture soaking the cotton of your panties and knowing that sitting close to me is making you wet causes my cock to continue to grow down my leg. I begin moving my finger up and down against your pussy through your panties. You close your eyes and breathe in deeply, a slight smile on your face. I continue to move my finger, massaging your clit through your panties and loving the expressions on your face as your excitement grows.

After several minutes, your rapid breathing and the glaze over your eyes tells me you are ready, and I begin to work my finger under the elastic of your panties. But you stop me, suddenly reaching down and grabbing my hand, pulling it away from your wetness. Still holding my hand, you rise from your seat and pull me from mine, almost dragging me. You head toward the elevators, pulling me behind you. When we get there, there are several others waiting.

The elevator arrives and we step in. You push me to the back and move directly in front of me, backing up tight to me and pressing your ass against my now raging cock. Others get on, the doors close and we begin to travel upwards. You begin to move your ass side to side, massaging my cock, driving me into a frenzy. I move my hand under your skirt and slip a finger through the T at the top of your thong. I slide it down the crack of your ass, pause briefly to finger your asshole and continue on down. My hand is cupping your ass and my middle finger moves to your clit, flicking it rapidly back and forth. You give an audible gasp and several people turn and glance quickly at you. Your pussy is soaking wet and my finger moves easily over you, circling your clit. The elevator moves slowly as we stop several times to let people off. I move the tip of my finger to your opening, which is drenched with your juices. Without hesitation, you push backwards against me and my finger slides easily all the way inside you.

© Martin Toye

With my palm against your ass, I fuck you with my finger and you bend ever so slightly at the waist to allow me better access, but not enough for the people with us to know *for sure* what is happening. I add a second finger and begin to finger-fuck you hard and fast and you sway your hips back and forth with the rhythm, barely noticeable. Your breathing is heavy and people are watching out of the corners of their eyes, but no one is brave enough to turn and look directly at us. I can see the flush on your cheeks, your eyes tightly closed, your teeth clenched, the muscles in your jaw standing out. I feel the muscles of your legs and stomach tighten and you reach behind you and grab both of my thigh muscles and squeeze tightly. I pump my fingers in and out of you faster and harder and your face turns bright red as your orgasm slams into you. You are holding your breath so forcefully to keep from screaming out. At that moment, the elevator stops on the 26th floor, the doors open and the last couple exits the elevator, leaving us alone. As the doors begin to close, they both look back at us just as your climax overpowers you and you scream out in ecstasy. Their eyes grow wide, jaws drop open and the door closes tight between us.

I pull my drenched fingers from your pussy and you turn, throw your arms around my neck and force your tongue into my mouth, kissing me deeply and passionately. You place your hand over my swollen cock and stroke it up and down through my pants. I move my fingers to our lips and slide them between our mouths and together, we lick your juices from them, tongues entwining around my fingers and around each other. You taste like heaven, even better than you do in my fantasies, and I can't wait to drink directly from your pussy. The elevator stops on 29, you grab my hand and once again pull me after you as we race to the room.

Once inside, we again turn to one another and our tongues entwine, wrestling furiously, holding each other desperately, pressing our bodies frantically together. Standing next to the bed, our mouths locked tightly together, we begin to undress each other…perhaps it would be more accurate to say we rip each other's clothes off. I push you back long enough to yank your top over your head before searching out your tongue once more. You grab the front of my shirt and wrench it apart, popping several buttons in the process. You push it back over my shoulders and it joins yours on the floor. My hands are at your breasts, desperately kneading, squeezing, pulling, pinching at your nipples. Your hands are on my chest, but quickly drop to my fly and you undo my pants, jerking them down over my ass and they slide down to the floor. As I step out of them, I reach under your skirt, grab the string of your thong and with one quick tug, the string snaps and they are on the floor. All that remains is your skirt and in one rapid motion, I pull it over your ass and it pools around your ankles.

I long to drink your body in with my eyes, seeing it for the first time, but I am incapable of separating my body, my lips, my hands from you. You push your tongue deeply into my mouth and I suck on it ravenously, my hands rapturous at the feel of your perfect ass as I squeeze it, my chest ecstatic at the feel of your perfect breasts pressed against it, my belly blissful at the feel of yours pushed against me. I hold you so tightly, so desperately, I cannot tell where your flesh ends and mine begins.

My mouth moves to your neck and I suck greedily at it, your head thrown back, your breaths coming hard and fast. You reach down and take my engorged cock, its tip red and angry, into your hand and begin to stroke me urgently up and down. My hand seeks out your sex once again, and when I find it, your saturated pussy sucks my fingers into you. My palm grinds against your clit as my fingers thrust in and out of you, making you pant and moan. Your frenzied pumping of my thick, throbbing cock has me so close to blasting all over your belly, but your belly is not where either one of us need my cum, so I push you away.

After the brief taste of your juices in the elevator, more than anything, I long to taste more of your pussy, but my cock is so enraged, straining so tightly against its own skin that I can think of nothing else except burying it inside you. I push you hard down on the bed, forcing a gasp from you. I climb over you and you immediately throw your legs wide and grab my cock, pulling me toward you. Without ceremony, the hunger evident on your face, you place the head of my cock against your soaked entrance, shove your hips up to me and your pussy swallows my entire cock in one stroke. The heat from your pussy is so intense and the feel of its walls squeezing my cock so tightly is so far beyond what I imagined it would be like to fuck you that I have to fight hard to keep from cumming instantly inside you. You gasp into my ear, "fuck me…fuck me hard…" and begin rocking your hips, forcing my cock in and out of you. I oblige and fuck you hard.

I grab your wrists and pull your hands over your head, gripping both with one hand and holding you there while my other hand pulls and pinches at your tits. My fully engorged cock stretches your pussy to its limits as it pounds in and out of you. You wrap your legs tightly around me and your ass rises off the bed with each stroke of my cock, slamming your mound into mine as we fuck. With each powerful stroke, you feel the length of my cock pressing against your swollen clit. You pull your hands free from my grip and grab my ass and frantically pull me hard into you with every plunge of my cock into your throbbing pussy. I can feel your fingernails digging into my ass and it makes me pump you relentlessly, thrusting deep into you over and over again. You grunt and moan and pant, bucking fiercely beneath me, your hips slamming into me, fucking me unmercifully. I move my hands under your ass, my weight holding you down hard. My hands grip your cheeks tightly, pulling you upwards, impaling you with my cock over and over again.

Your eyes begin to roll back in your head, your fingernails gouge my ass, your body shudders beneath me and the scream starts deep in your chest. I feel the intensity building, first in my balls, then in the pit of my stomach. My cock thrusts in and out of your pussy and this time, it's my turn to say, my mouth against your ear…"fuck me…fuck me…you're gonna make me cum so hard…fuck me…fuck me hard….*fuck me*…FUCK ME…*FUCK ME*…**FUCK ME!**"

The scream in your chest moves into your throat and as you thrash violently beneath me, my cock slamming hard into you, I feel your pussy beginning its convulsions as you start to cum, contracting tightly around my cock. My orgasm smashes into me full force and my entire body begins to spasm over you. I scream out as my hot cum shoots inside you, your juices run down my balls and together, we explode furiously. Your arms are wrapped so tightly around me I can hardly breathe as you buck violently beneath me. We buck and thrash and shudder uncontrollably as wave after wave washes over us, all the while, my cock slamming into your dripping wet pussy, your pussy convulsing around my spurting cock, rearing up off the bed to take me deeper, every muscle, every nerve twitching as we cum and cum and cum and cum. Just when I think I have nothing left, your pulsating pussy milks a little more from me, and with each pulse, your body spasms in ecstasy. We collapse in each other's arms, totally spent, incapable of movement, wallowing in our euphoria.

Fantasy girl, the first time I fuck you *has* to be hard, fast, frantic, violent. And when I have the strength to raise my head, it is then that I will revel in your body, touching, kissing, licking every inch of it. It is then that I will place my tongue against your pussy and take you to heaven, as many times as you would like to visit. It is then that I will make love to you, moving my cock slowly and passionately in and out of you, making it last as long as I can for you, teasing you, bringing you close and finally taking you there. It is then that I will take hours to please you. But the first time we fuck, it will be over in seconds, but it will be seconds like neither of us has ever experienced before.

TWO FIRES – PART ONE

Hello, my beautiful fantasy girl. I know how you like it. I know that you would rather be fucked hard, pinned against the wall, bodies sweaty and pounding, but if you don't mind, I think I would rather make love to you today. I promise that I will fuck you so hard you will burst your vocal cords screaming in ecstasy another day. Today, I need a fireplace, a bottle of wine and a good movie. Please sweetheart, will you curl up with me? Figuratively that is...the fireplace is burning, but I'm going to skip the wine and the movie if that's okay with you.

I dream of you on a chilly evening, sitting close together on the couch in front of the fireplace. The only light is coming from the fire, warming your skin and giving you a soft glow. You look so beautiful sitting there next to me, your hair reflecting the brilliance of the fire, your skin bronze and glowing. I place my hand against your cheek and lean in to you and our lips touch for the first time, your lips soft and smooth, your breath sweet. You part your lips and your tongue touches mine, circling the tip of my tongue slowly and gently. Your hand rests on my thigh and mine cradles your head behind your ear, my fingertips rubbing gently at the back of your head. I pull you closer and you begin to kiss me more deeply, our tongues moving together in tender rhythm.

I move my hand to your hip and I feel your hand beginning to move slowly and lightly against my thigh. I slide my hand up your side, my thumb along your belly until it reaches the underside of your breast. I pause there, but your kisses become deeper and your hand tightens on my thigh and I know you are ready for my touch, that you desire my touch. I move my hand up under your arm and my thumb rises over the swell of your breast and briefly touches your nipple. You inhale sharply and squeeze my thigh again and I begin to draw circles around your nipple with my thumb. Your body responds by leaning in closer to me and your hand moves up my inner thigh. My thumb moves back and forth over your nipple and I can feel it swelling at my touch, just as my cock is beginning to swell in my pants. Your hand inches up my thigh and my cock inches towards your hand as it grows until at last they meet. You move your thumb back and forth over the head of my cock through my pants, just as my thumb is moving back and forth over your nipple.

I slide my hand under your top and caress your perfect belly with the palm of my hand. I move up to your bare breast and cup it in my hand, my palm rubbing circles against your nipple. You reach for my fly and open my pants, taking out my cock. You wrap your hand around it, rubbing your thumb over its head and then begin to stroke it slowly up and down, bringing it to its full extension. Your hand feels so good around me and you can hear my breathing becoming more rapid at your touch. I take your nipple between my thumb and finger and pull at it lightly, feeling it growing harder at my touch. With your hand still stroking my cock, I move my hand to your thigh and slide it up your skirt until I reach the triangle of cotton at the top. I rub one finger over your panties and can feel the heat and dampness of your pussy through them. You feel your clit beginning to swell at my touch and I rub my finger up and down it. You move your hips against my touch and I slide my finger underneath the cotton and place the tip of my finger against your clit and flick it back and forth lightly. Your quickened breathing and your hand's faster movement up and down on my cock tells me you are ready for more.

Pushing you back on the couch, I pull your skirt down over your legs, followed by your panties. You quickly pull your top off and lay back on the couch. You feel my eyes burning over your body, drinking in your perfection...the narrow expanse of waist, the enticing slope of hip as it dissolves into your exquisite belly, the curve of your perfect breasts, your legs stretched out before me, so perfect and toned...the legs of a goddess, across your thin ankles and then, your beautiful feet. I watch you for a moment in awe of your perfection and feel a tear welling, just as I do when I am standing before any truly magnificent work of art, all of which pale next to your beauty. You are truly breathtaking in the most literal sense of the word...watching you lying there makes it hard for me to breathe.

© Steve Anderson Photography

You part your legs slightly for me and show me your beautiful pussy for the first time. Again, I cannot help but stare at how beautiful and perfect it is, your clit now swollen and peeking out from between your lips, glistening with moisture. I reach out and spread your lips with my thumb and first finger, exposing your button further, and with the middle finger of my other hand, I begin to circle your clit. You throw one leg over the back of the couch and place your other foot on the floor, opening yourself wide to my touch. Pulling your lips back, I press the tip of my finger directly on your clit and begin to gyrate it rapidly back and forth, forcing a gasp from you. You begin to squirm and your breath is coming in pants. My finger moves faster and faster over your clit and it is now as hard and round as a marble. I push harder against it, moving my finger back and forth, varying the velocity until I can tell from your reaction that I've found the perfect rhythm. Your panting turns to moans and you begin to pinch your nipples frantically, while my finger presses firmly against your clit. Your stomach muscles tighten and a growl begins to grow in your chest.

I watch your face in fascination as your climax grows, both your teeth and your eyes clenched tightly closed, your face beginning to flush. You arch your back and lift your ass high off the couch and just as you start to cum, I slide two fingers into your wet, convulsing pussy and you scream out. I fuck you hard, fingers pumping in and out of you and pushing urgently against your clit. You reach down and grab my wrist with both hands and pump my hand harder and faster in and out of you, bucking against me and screaming out loud. The heels of your hands are pressing my finger even tighter against your clit as you continue to pull my hand in and out of your pussy. You throw your head back, no longer breathing, your face turning red, eyes clenched tightly shut, the cords in your neck standing out as the power of your orgasm sensitizes every nerve. Your entire body begins to shake uncontrollably and at long last, you fall back onto the couch, completely spent and gasping.

I watch you lying there, red faced and panting for breath, and can't help but smile, knowing how hard I just made you cum. I slide my fingers gently from your pussy and put them to my mouth, tasting your sweet juices and breathing you in. You open your eyes and watch me sucking your cum from my fingers and smile at me. Your eyes close again, but the smile remains on your face. I bend over, my face between your legs and blow softly against your clit, the cool air soothing the burning in your abused pussy. You give a little moan of pleasure and tell me not to stop. The cool air is causing a tingle in your sex and you reach down and begin to caress my cheek. I hear you say "mmmm, that feels so good" and you begin to run your fingers through my hair. I feel your hand on the back of my head and you begin to pull me gently toward you.

© Martin Toye

To be continued…

THE MUSIC MAN

He plays from his heart
Fingers alive on the strings
Drawing from the instrument
The melody he gives wings

His eyes are closed in concentration
Relying on touch to find the way
Tentative, then confident
He feels, then starts to play.

His fingers glide softly across the strings
Causing the ripples he desires
His caress brings forth the first sounds
Of sweetness, warmth and light.

And now the music moves him
With its slow caress
His touch awakens the melody
That's been so long at rest.

The melody, now awakened,
Blossoms at his touch
Spreading her blooms around him
Petals, rich and lush.

The melody guides him into her
As his hands continue to coax
The sweet music from her depths
Oh, those sweet, sweet notes!

He moves slowly across the strings
Feeling each delicious note
The movement of the music
Takes him deeper with each stroke.

The melody is all that matters
He thinks of nothing more
He coaxes sounds before unheard
From the instrument he adores.

He moves in perfect rhythm
To the music of his soul
His instrument is weeping
Seeking heaven's goal.

His caress becomes more urgent
As the passion of his play
Ignites the fire of heartstrings
And desire overtakes.

His fingers fly across the strings
Driving to crescendo
The melody begins to swell
Arching up to meet him.

The music throbs, the music crashes
As thunder's passion storm
Threatening to engulf them
With an ecstasy all its own.

Desperately, frantically, urgently
The melody pulls him deeper
Her petals grip him tightly
As the finale builds within her.

He brings forth from this instrument
A climax of sound so fine
Wave after wave crashes over them
Breathless, euphoric, divine.

Never has such a melody
Blossomed in such full bloom
Never has his touch before
Brought forth this melodic tune.

Now with his symphony complete
He stands for his curtain call
He opens his eyes and is saddened to see
All this time, he's been alone.

He dreams of a day when he can coax
This beautiful melody
From the instrument he longs to play,
And does, in fantasy.

DRESSING YOU

Samarel

Hey fantasy girl. I dreamed of you again last night. In my dream, we were in the city shopping together. When I woke up, my excitement to see you again was VERY evident, so I closed my eyes and relived it...

We are in your favorite clothing store and you are dressed in the most amazing outfit...tight little belly shirt that accentuates your gorgeous tits and shows off your perfect belly, a cute little skirt just barely covers your incredible ass, high heeled strappy shoes that do things to your legs and feet that just aren't possible outside of the imagination. The store is crowded and everyone you pass can't help but stare. Panties are damp and cocks are straining against material everywhere you walk.

You pull tiny little sexy outfits off the rack and hold them up to your body to ask me what I think. As I imagine you in each one, my cock begins to grow. You notice the swelling in my pants, give a mischievous little smile, step close to me, trace your fingers over the outline of my cock and whisper in my ear "I want to fuck...NOW!" I take your hand and lead you to the back of the store to the dressing rooms. The attendant's back is turned and I pull you quickly into the only unoccupied room and close the door behind us.

I push you into the corner and we begin to kiss, furiously and urgently. My hands are on your tits, squeezing and pulling at your nipples while your hand rubs frantically at my cock through my pants. I grab your leg behind the knee and pull it up to my waist. You wrap it around me and begin to ride my thigh, your pussy grinding into me. I reach my hand down and cup your ass. As is typical, you aren't wearing any panties and I slide my hand under you and begin to finger your clit while you push against me. Your pussy is so hot and wet. I slide a finger in you and begin to fuck you with it while you moan and grind against my thigh.

© Martin Toye

You reach down and undo my pants, releasing my cock, and begin to stroke me hard and fast. I am rock hard now and your expert hand soon has me ready to unload all over your belly. I pull your hand away, grab your other leg behind the knee and lift you up off the ground. My cock is wedged between my belly and your clit and with both hands on your ass, I raise you up and down, pulling you hard against me and rubbing your clit up and down the entire length of my cock, your pussy juices soaking it. You are moaning softly with your face buried in my shoulder. I raise you up until the tip of my cock is even with your opening and you reach around behind, take my cock in your hand and align the head of it with your hot, wet slit. I slowly lower you onto my cock until I am all the way deep inside you. I lift you off my cock until only the very tip is still inside you and then let you drop back down on it, hard and fast. At this angle, your clit rubs against my cock from top to bottom with every stroke as I lift you up and down on it. You are moaning loudly now, but don't care who hears. My hands are tight on your ass, squeezing your cheeks hard, lifting you up and down faster and faster, my cock now slamming into your tight pussy. You are panting and rocking against me, your arms tight around my neck, jumping up and down on my cock. I can feel your pussy beginning to tighten which takes me to the edge. I lean you back into the corner and pump you even harder as I feel my orgasm building. I feel your pussy beginning to spasm and you bite down hard into my shoulder to keep from screaming as you begin to cum. Just as the first wave hits you, I slide a finger into your ass and begin to fuck your ass with the same hard rhythm of the pounding of my cock in your pussy. You scream out and explode, your nails digging into my back, your heels digging into the back of my thighs, your teeth digging into my shoulder. The intensity of your orgasm brings me over the top and my cock explodes into you so hard you can feel my load pumping into you.

Your entire body begins to shake with the force of your orgasm and I continue to slam my cock into you, my finger fucking your ass hard and fast. Wave after explosive wave takes you and you cum and cum again. You throw your head back, your mouth wide open in a scream, but there is no sound left in you as you quiver and spasm around my cock, your climax still washing over you. Our fucking is starting to slow now, both of us weak from our explosive orgasms, but your clit is still rubbing against my shaft as my cock continues to stretch the walls of your pussy and you are whimpering softly in my ear. The force of my ejaculation has my knees so weak, I can no longer hold you. I lower you to the ground and collapse against you, only the wall holding us up.

Sweetheart, I have to end the telling of my fantasy dream here because I just came so hard I don't have the strength to continue writing. But when at last we meet, I think a trip to the mall may be in order.

A TASTE OF FANTASY

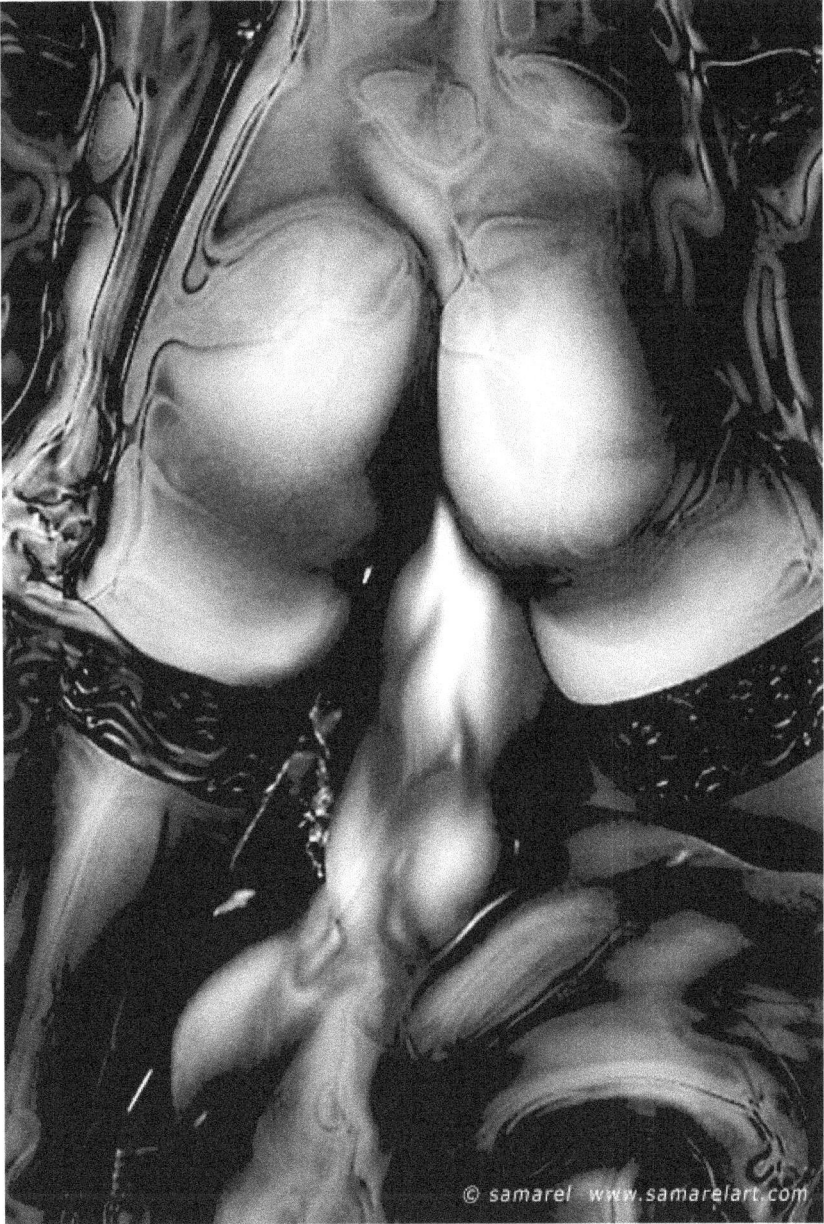

© samarel www.samarelart.com

Good morning, fantasy girl. I'm thinking of you right now, lying before me on this big, king-size bed. I dream of feeling your lips against mine, gently, softly, passionately, tongues lightly touching, tongues drawing circles on each other, tongues entwined, lips pressing frantically...god, I love to kiss you!

While kissing you, I dream of cupping your breasts in my hand, squeezing gently, sliding my palm over them, taking your nipples between my thumb and forefinger and massaging softly, squeezing them, pinching them, pulling hard at them, feeling them swell until hard as a little stone.

But most of all, I dream of watching your face, looking up at you from between your legs as you arch your back, throw your head back and scream out loud as my tongue presses against your clit, my fingers sliding in and out of your pussy. Can I take you there now? Will you let me make you cum? Over and over again?

We lie on the bed, you on your back and me leaning over you, kissing passionately, my hand at your breasts, yours fondling my cock. I take my lips from yours, moving down your neck, sucking and biting for a moment before continuing to your breasts. My tongue circles your nipples, my teeth nibble at them, pull at them. I move further down your belly, kissing it everywhere, slipping my tongue into your belly button.

I settle between your legs, my arms under you, my hands curling up over the top of your thighs and I grasp you with both hands and spread your legs. I don't have to exert much effort as you willingly move them as far apart as you can, exposing your beautiful pussy to me. My lips find your inner thighs and I begin to kiss them gently and softly, moving from thigh to thigh, teasing, licking, kissing. My lips and tongue caress your flesh where your legs meet your sex, so close to the lips of your pussy, but being careful not to touch them. I tease you with my tongue at the curve of the start of your ass, I slide it up alongside your sex...up one side and down the other, always close but never quite touching. You begin to squirm beneath me, shifting from side to side, trying to find my mouth with your pussy. But I only tease, my tongue now traveling up over your mound at the uppermost tip of your slit and back down your inner thigh. As your juices begin to flow, your erotic scent taunts me as much as my tongue taunts you and I can't wait any longer to taste you.

As my lips move from one thigh to the other, I flick out my tongue and barely touch the tip of it to your clit as I pass by. You gasp and grab the back of my head, trying to guide my tongue to you. I allow you to guide me and place the tip of my tongue against the sensitive patch of flesh between your pussy and asshole and slowly and gently slide it upwards, over your lips, skimming lightly over your clit, barely touching you. My touch is so light you can barely feel it, just a tickle against the folds of your pussy. When I reach the top, I slide slowly back down, all the way to your ass and I tongue your pink asshole briefly before starting my way back up again. The tip of my tongue tickles up and down your sex, lightly, slowly, gently, up...and down...and up...and down...and up...and down. Can you feel it, sweetie? Can you feel my tongue sliding oh so slowly over you? Can you feel it tickle your sex? Is your clit getting as hard as my cock is right now?

As my tongue reaches your puckered pink hole again, I press ever so slightly and begin working my way back up, my tongue parting your lips as it travels upwards. The tip of my tongue moves slowly up over your delicious opening, enjoying its wetness, and then between your lips to the right of your clit, up to the very uppermost tip of your sex and then back down along the left side. As the tip works its way into your folds, the side of my tongue rubs against your clit as I move up and down on you. You moan softly as my tongue continues its slow journey, just inside your lips on each side of your button. Your pussy is drenched from your juices and mine and the path is slick and smooth for the tip of my tongue. I circle your clit slowly, sometimes brushing slightly against it, sometimes lingering at your sweetest of openings, always gently, always slowly, always wet. After long minutes of slow, wet pressure up and down your pink flesh, I pull back and blow gently against your sex, directing a stream of cool breath directly onto your now swollen clit. You moan and again try to pull my head back into your pussy.

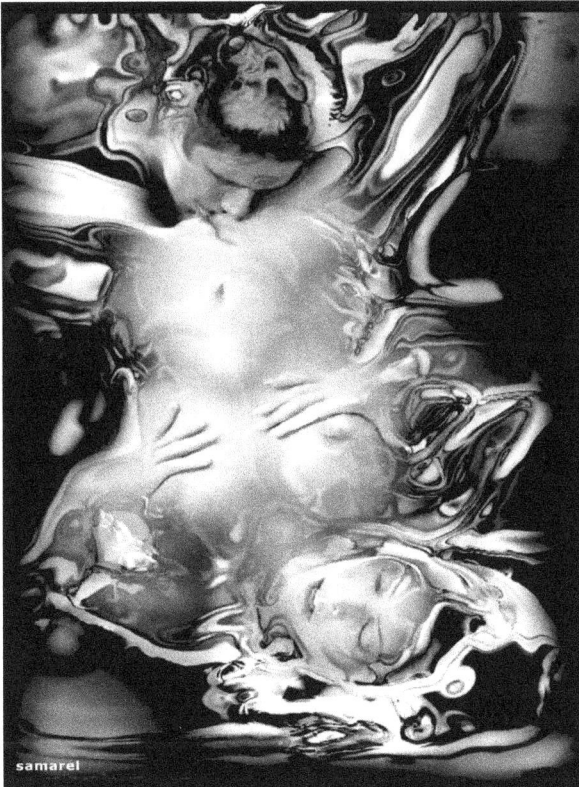

samarel

Your soft moans, your gently arching back, your hands at the back of my head all tell me that you are ready for more and I love to oblige. With my arms still under your thighs and my hands wrapped over the top of your legs, I softly place my fingertips against the lips of your pussy and pull them gently apart, fully exposing your clit. My mouth is so close you can feel my hot breath against your clit and you pull my head toward you and press your sex towards my face.

My tongue shoots out and flicks your clit...once...twice...now rapidly flicking against it, directly on the tiny hole at its base. My fingers spread your lips further and your swollen clit stands straight out, fully erect as the tip of my tongue flicks it over and over again. You try to press your pussy into my face, but I'm not ready for that and pull back, the tip of my tongue never leaving your clit, never ceasing its rapid movement, like hummingbird wings against your clit, only wet and hot. Your moans are no longer soft, the arch of your back no longer gentle, your hands now desperate at the back of my head, pulling me, grinding your pussy into my face. But still, the flicking continues, frenzied and unrelenting.

I move my arms over the tops of your thighs and place the fingers of both hands at the top of your mound, pulling upwards and stretching the flesh of your sex tight, raising and exposing your clit even further. I give in to your need and place my tongue hard against it and begin to rub it up and down with my tongue, pulling back on your mound as I press against your clit with the meat of my tongue. My upper lip presses hard against you as I rub your clit, hard and fast, up and down and up and down. It has become hard and round as a little stone and I work it furiously, enjoying you squirming beneath me, loving your hands pressing hard to the back of my head, savoring your sweet scent as you grind your clit against my tongue, your juices running down my chin.

Your clit grows harder as you get closer to cumming. My tongue presses against you frantically and you raise your hips completely off the bed, grinding your pussy into my face. You pull my head so hard into your sex that I can barely breathe, but it doesn't stop my tongue and as the first wave hits you, you begin to rock against my face, desperately pulling me into you and grinding hard against my tongue. You scream out and your entire body begins to convulse, but my tongue never leaves your clit, pressing urgently up and down, back and forth. Your feet are under you now and you are pressing your pussy so hard into my face and rocking against my tongue, cumming long and hard and drenching my face with your juices. I drink you in and your body gives one last tremendous spasm before falling back onto the bed.

I pull back and blow cool air onto your pussy, attempting to cool your burning clit. You move your hands from the back of my head and slide them down between your legs, taking your pussy lips between your fingers and spreading them to speed the cooling. Instead, I slip my tongue back onto your clit and begin to flick it lightly again. Your lower body begins to shake uncontrollably, but you don't stop me. Instead, you pull your lips back even further from your clit and I know that you are ready for more. I never disappoint. You bend your knees and pull your legs up, fully exposing your pussy and ass to me. My tongue begins to travel up and down from your clit to your asshole and back again. Up and down, slowly but firmly.

I pause at your ass and tongue you there, tasting the juices that flowed from your last orgasm. I watch as you slip one finger over your clit and rub it rapidly back and forth as my tongue works its way slowly into your ass, spreading your tight hole as it moves deeper into you. Your moans begin again and you bend your knees to your chest, trying to give more of your ass to my tongue. When it has reached as deep as it can go, I slide it slowly back out, back in, back out, now a bit faster, now a bit deeper, fucking your ass with my tongue. Your finger moves furiously over your clit, but not willing to give up my greatest pleasure, my mouth moves back up and I push your hand away with my nose as my tongue takes over for your finger. Again, you spread your lips for me, leaving my hands free to do other things that I NEED to do to you.

My tongue works over your clit, pressing against it, moving rapidly up and down over it, using my entire tongue to cover every inch of you. Your fingers are at the inside of your lips on each side of your clit and I can feel you pressing hard as my tongue works you, sliding over you, hot and wet. I place one finger over your opening and slowly work it into your pussy while my tongue pushes against your clit and you begin to grind into my face once again. My finger moves easily in and out of you and I press the roof of your pussy with my fingertip, sliding it back and forth in rhythm with my tongue.

You begin to moan again and when I add a second finger, your moaning becomes loud and your breathing harsh. As my tongue works your clit, I fuck you with two fingers, moving them deeply in and out of you, your pussy gripping them tightly as I begin to move faster inside you. Can you feel them? Can you feel my fingers inside you, stroking and probing and circling?

Your fingers are on each side of my tongue, pressing inside your lips as my tongue works you into a frenzy. You shove your pussy into my face, grinding hard into it. Your ass is still pulled high into the air and you begin to rock against my tongue. Suddenly, I suck your clit into my mouth and begin to pull hard on it. You begin to shake and a growl builds in your throat, growing louder and louder. I suck harder at your clit, circling it inside my mouth with my tongue, pulling it tight with my lips, my fingers slamming into your pussy, hard and fast, in and out, pounding and gyrating. You grab the backs of your knees and pull your legs tightly to your chest and grind your pussy hard into my face, rocking against the fingers that are pounding you so frantically. Just as your growl reaches its peak, I slip a finger into your ass and finger-fuck your ass and pussy together as you grind into my face and I suck hard on your clit. You scream out, loud and long, exploding violently, every muscle of your pussy and ass pulsating tightly around my fingers. Your clit feels as swollen and large as a marble as I suck it hard into my mouth. Your entire body begins to convulse, bucking up and down on the bed, as you cum and cum and cum, waves of ecstasy slamming into you over and over again. Your screams of pleasure are deafening, my fingers unrelenting, my tongue unceasing and the waves continue to pound you, every nerve in your body cumming all at the same time.

Cum for me, my love...cum hard for me...cum with me...right now...

THAT SMILE

samarelart.com

You look back over your shoulder and give me that mischievous smile of yours, wiggling your perfect ass at me, taunting me, saying "come fuck me now" without ever opening your mouth. I sit and watch you, bent over before me, staring at your ass, feeling my desire and my cock grow.

You reach down through your legs and place your middle fingertip against your asshole and drag it slowly down over your pussy, parting your lips for me as you go, causing your clit to peek out at me. There's that smile again, taunting me. Your finger travels back to your ass, over your pussy, parting your lips, baring your clit, back to your ass, over your pussy...

That smile, that "fuck me" smile.

You shift from one foot to the other and I watch as your ass moves in rhythm with the shift. You watch over your shoulder as I lean back in my chair, undo my fly and pull out my cock...long, thick, veined and rigid. I watch you lick your lips...I see the hunger in your eyes as you stare at my engorged cock. You arch your back and circle your hips, tormenting me with your ass. I move my hand to my cock and you watch me as I stroke it slowly up and down.

Your finger is now moving faster over your pussy, burrowed between your lips, rubbing your clit back and forth. You reach back and put your other hand on your cheek, spreading your ass for me, showing me your pink, puckered opening, showing me your juices glistening on your finger. Still, that devilish smile. I need to fuck that smile off your face.

I rise and step up behind you, my cock still in my hand, angry and throbbing. You move your ass from side to side, continuing to taunt me, continuing to make me insane with desire. With both hands, you reach between your legs and with your hands high up on your thighs and your fingers on each side of your sex, you spread it wide for me, showing me the delicious pink of the inside of your pussy...shiny, glistening, pulsing. You arch your back further, shoving your ass out toward me.

I can't resist your ass there before me, sticking out, teasing me. You need to be taught a lesson. The flat of my hand resounds against your ass as I smack it hard...SLAP! You gasp in surprise but recover immediately and whisper "again...harder". My hand finds your ass again...SMACK!... firm and loud. I move one hand to the small of your back, pushing downward, forcing your ass higher into the air. Over and over, I swat your ass, watching it turn red, listening to you pant, listening to you beg for more. With each slap, I become more aroused, more enraged and the spanking turns furious...urgent. I am so lost in my desire, it is long moments before I hear you crying out for me to stop, begging me for release.

I step back, breathing hard, shocked at how red and swollen your ass has become. You move your hands over it gently, trying to soothe the burn. Yet I can see that your pussy is dripping wet and I hear you panting with desire.

I step behind you, my cock standing straight out, threatening to burst from its skin. Your hands move back to your thighs and again, you stretch your pussy wide for me. The tip of my cock is directly against your opening. You shove back against me, surprising me, unready for you and it is my turn to gasp at the pleasure of your steaming sex swallowing the head of my cock. You shove back a second time, and my raging cock is buried deep inside you.

Your pussy is so tight, so wet, so hot, I moan out loud. I begin moving my cock in and out of you and your moans join mine. I can feel that beautiful bundle of flesh inside your pussy against the head of my cock and I know that I am driving directly against your g-spot. It fans my fire further and I plunge my cock deep into you, feeling your ass slamming against my belly. You are too tight...I can't stand it...you are gripping me so tightly. I'm going to cum so hard inside you.

I lean over you, laying my chest on your back, and reach around and place my hand between your legs. I feel your swollen clit and take it between my fingers. With my other hand, I grab your tits, pinching and pulling at your nipples. My cock is thrusting in and out of you, stretching the walls of your pussy, making you moan with pleasure. You are so tight around me, you feel every vein of my cock as it pounds into your pussy. I stroke your clit hard with my fingers and stroke your sex hard with my cock. You have me so close...I'm afraid to move...not yet...don't make me cum yet. You push your ass back hard against me, rocking your hips, taking control, fucking me. I feel your pussy begin to tighten around me…you feel my cock swelling inside you. You are going to make me cum so hard!

I stand up straight, grab your hair and pull your head back and slam my cock hard into your g-spot. I scream out in ecstasy as I shoot hot cum against it. You scream with me, your climax hitting you, my cock pounding you so frantically, waves of pleasure washing over you. Your pussy convulses around my cock, pumping me, milking the cum from me. My fingers grind against your engorged clit, my cock thrusts hard into you, my hand pulling hard at your hair, bending you back. Your juices flood my cock, running down my balls as they slap your clit with each pounding stroke. Your legs begin to shake involuntarily, your ass bucks against my belly, your pussy clenches around my cock as you continue to cum and cum. I love to feel you spasm uncontrollably around my cock and it prolongs my orgasm, just as my pulsing, pounding cock prolongs yours. Finally, my cock completely drained, I collapse onto your back, our juices overflowing and dripping to the floor.

Raising your head, you look back at me over your shoulder. Your smile is still there…I couldn't fuck it off your face. But it's a different smile…a beautiful smile, a content smile, the smile of a woman in love. That's really all I wanted.

COME, SHE WROTE *(written by Fantasy Girl)*

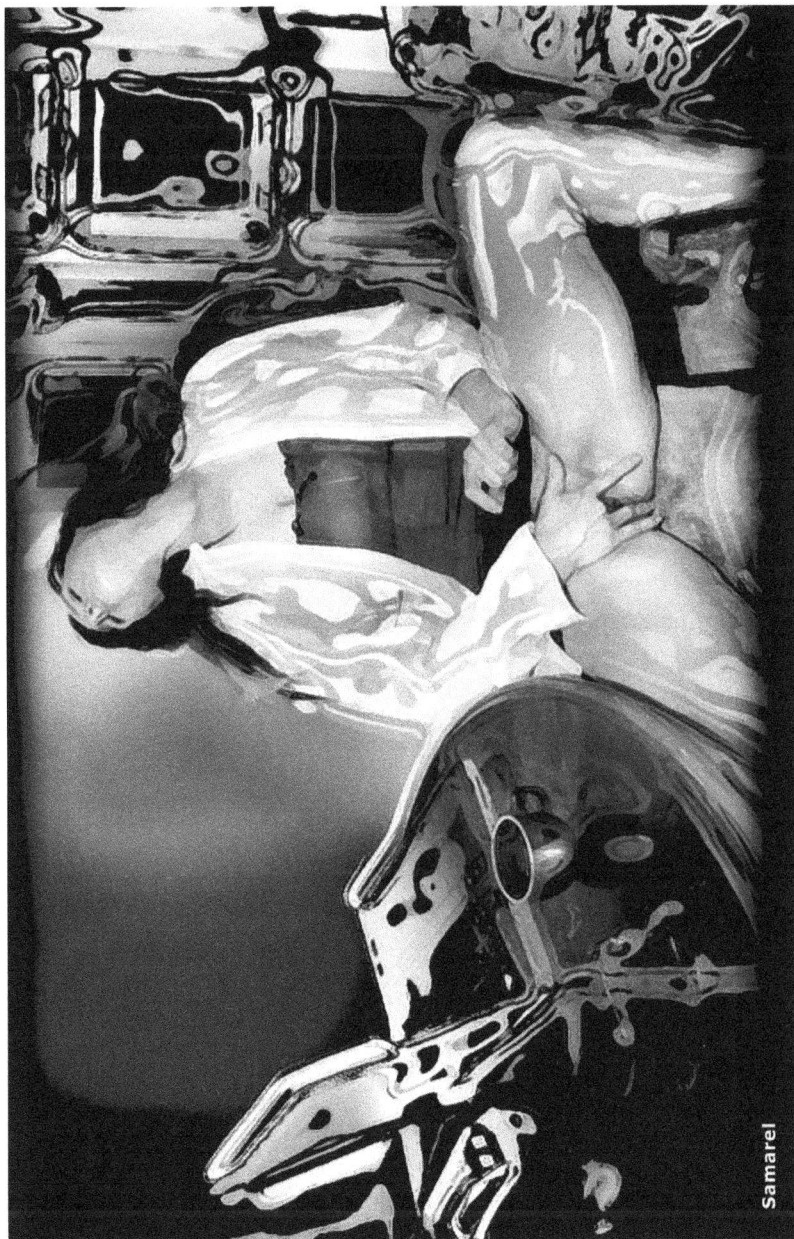

I've been thinking about you. Wondering about you really. I had two glasses of wine and could not help but wonder what you're doing… whether you're stroking your cock to thoughts of me. How many times did you fuck me today, and in how many ways? Mmmm. You intrigue me, you arouse me, you make me wet knowing that you're so close. Just a small distance away, only separated by this screen. It sends shivers down my spine to know you could be reading this at the same time I am. That you could be masturbating with me as our eyes follow my words. That your hand is matching my rhythm as we touch ourselves.

Do you wonder the same? Do you *feel* the same way? It's so vivid. I can imagine you there, your hand slowly stroking yourself, arousing yourself while you read. I want to be there. I want to watch you... I want you to watch me. Voyeurs together. Would you want that? Do you want to see my fingers on my clit? My hand around my breast, pinching my nipple? Do you want to see the way my back arches? The look on my face when I cum? I want to look into your eyes to know you're watching me. I want to watch your movements, your hand moving against yourself, the arching of your back, hear the small noises you make as you bring yourself closer.

Just thinking about this has me touching myself. I've slid my hand down into my panties, letting my fingers drift softly over me. I'm already wet. You arouse me so very much. My fingers slide down my slit, spreading my wetness. I can't believe how wet you have me, how aroused my body is. I'm sliding them back up, back and forth, rubbing my velvety lips with my fingertips. So wet. Pushing a finger slowly inside me... oh God, I need this so much. Stroking myself with it, rubbing the way I like. I wish you could see me, hear me...

These jeans need to come off. My panties are soaked. Should I take them off too? I think you'd rather like that. Maybe my shirt and bra as well....

I can see my reflection in the screen. It's a sensual picture. I wish you could see me this way. I've put one foot up against the desk, spreading my thighs. I want to take a picture of myself like this for you, but I don't want to stop. I need to keep touching myself. I want to cum for you... with you.

I'm pushing my fingers back down my slit, two fingers this time, sliding into me. My other fingers are on my nipple, pinching it hard, increasing my arousal. I can hear how wet I am... can you hear me? The sound of my fingers sliding in and out of my dripping wet pussy?

© Martin Toye

God, I want you. I want you to be able to hear me. I want you to be able to hear everything, all of my sounds, my moans, my gasps. I'm stroking faster, pushing harder. I can feel my muscles tightening around my fingers... so close...

Tell me. Tell me you're masturbating with me, tell me how good it feels, arouse me more. I need to hear you telling me that you're close too, that you want to cum too.

God, I need to touch my clit... I want to keep typing but I don't know if I can. It's too much, I want to cum for you. I want you to know how much I need that... I'm so fucking close now, my breath is ragged...

I need my vibrator. I'm taking it out of the drawer, letting it rub against my wetness, coating it with my juices. Up and down, rubbing it against me. Pushing it inside me... pushing you inside me... so thick and full, filling me. That's what I needed, so close now. Pushing it deep inside me, thrusting into my pussy, fucking myself with it. My thumb on my clit, rubbing it hard, yes, circling it around and around... fuck, yes... thrusting it harder, faster... I need to cum. Tell me you want me to cum... please, I need to hear it from you, to hear your voice telling me to cum for you...

Oh God, that's it, the heat's moving through me. I can feel it between my thighs. A radiating heat growing in me, building, pulsing... I can feel it flushing up my neck, up to my face. Rubbing faster, that's it, there, God... now... I'm going to cum now, cum with me, please, I want you to cum with me, oh God...

Is it any wonder she's my fantasy girl?

TWO FIRES – PART TWO

www.samarelart.com

... I hear you say "mmmm, that feels so good" and you begin to run your fingers through my hair. I feel your hand on the back of my head and you begin to pull me gently toward you.

I kiss your inner thighs, licking your sweet juices from them. I savor your taste as my tongue moves from thigh to thigh, to the curve of your ass, over the fleshy folds surrounding your pussy, licking up every drop of your cum. You move your hands from the back of my head and take your knees in your hands, drawing them up to your chest, pulling your ass into the air and fully exposing your perfect pussy and your gorgeous ass to my lips. I clean your love juices from your cheeks with my tongue and find myself wallowing in your beautiful ass, rubbing my face all over it. With your knees still raised to your chest, you reach back and spread your cheeks, exposing your beautiful pink, puckered button to me. My tongue finds the sensitive spot directly beneath your pussy and I linger there, licking and teasing it. But I can't resist any longer and move down an inch and begin to tongue your ass, circling it gently, loving the feel of it against my lips and tongue. You are moaning softly again and I watch as you move one hand to your pussy and begin to massage your clit with your finger. Your finger moves slowly and seductively, teasing your clit. Watching you touch yourself is so erotic and my cock is straining against its own skin.

I move upward and press my lips to you, flicking my tongue out and touching the flesh of your mound. Your scent is utterly intoxicating and I revel in it, my tongue teasing you, making you crazy with want. My lips move over you, my tongue working each side of your pussy where your thighs meet your body. Up one side, over the top of your mound and back down the other, slowly circling your beautiful pink pussy. You tighten your grip on my head and begin to push me towards your sex, your desire now strong. I breathe you in and your aroma causes my cock to throb with desire. I release my tongue, just barely touching it against your clit and your body shivers. I slide it gently over your clit, drawing tiny circles on it with the very tip of my tongue. It finds the tiny little spot directly below your button and works its way into it, then slides up over your tiny knob and back down, gently, softly, slowly. I can feel your clit swelling now and I increase the pressure of my tongue against it just ever so slightly. Your hips rotate slowly, keeping time with my tongue sliding up and down on your button.

I move one hand between your legs and touch your opening with the tip of my finger, rubbing it gently as my tongue continues on your clit. The tip of my tongue is barely touching you and I begin to flick it rapidly, causing you to inhale sharply and another "mmmm..." escapes your lips. My tongue never tires and I continue to flick it against your clit for many long minutes, my finger exploring the edge of your opening, drawing circles on it. Your breathing quickens and your button is enflamed and swollen against my tongue. My tongue parts your lips as I press my thumb against your mound at the top of your slit and put pressure there, pulling back and stretching your pussy tight. Your hands are at the back of my head and you pull me desperately against you.

My tongue is pressing firmly against your clit, the tip buried against your tiny urinary opening. You pull my head tighter into you and push your pussy brutally against my tongue and rock your hips. My tongue moves up and down on your clit, pressing harder and harder, moving faster and faster. Your moans grow louder as my tongue drives you wild with desire. Your hips buck hard against my face as you grind your pussy into my tongue. My finger moves faster against your opening and I suddenly slide it inside you, making your entire body wrench. You fuck my finger violently as my tongue pushes against your clit, my thumb pulling back and stretching your flesh tight. You grind harder and harder into my tongue and breathe out "two fingers...two fingers", panting harshly and rocking against my face.

I slide a second finger into you, reaching deep inside you and I find that tiny bundle of flesh inside your pussy and begin to slide the tips of my fingers over it rapidly, pushing hard against it and sliding back and forth over it while my tongue presses against your clit. Your moans are coming rapidly and growing louder and louder, your hands at the back of my head pulling me into you so hard, my tongue grinding against your clit, my fingers fucking you furiously. You shout out "you're gonna make me cum...make me cum...fuck me...fuck me...FUCK ME!"

You arch your back, grinding your pussy into my face, and scream out as your orgasm pounds you, causing your entire body to jerk spasmodically. You buck uncontrollably against my face, forcing my tongue hard against your clit, forcing my fingers deep inside your pussy and I pump them in and out of you. Your clit is throbbing against my tongue and your pussy is clenching my fingers tightly. Clenching and releasing, clenching and releasing, in the throes of ecstasy that are washing over you. You cum violently and keep cumming, grinding your clit against my tongue, my fingers fucking you hard and fast, spasms contorting your body.

Just as your climax begins to subside, I shove my fingers deep into your pussy and press against your g-spot and another wave shoots through your body, making you scream out in pleasure as another orgasm explodes over you. Over and over, I plunge deep into your pussy. Over and over, I force my tongue harder against your clit. Over and over, you explode in orgasm, your entire body shaking and spasming, your arms tight around my head, squeezing my face into your pussy. With a final convulsion, wildly bucking against my face, you let loose a final orgasmic scream and collapse into the couch, your body quivering unwillingly.

You are barely able to move, every muscle in your body completely limp as the fire crackles in the fireplace. But I'm not through with you yet. The violence of your cumming has my cock so screaming hard and I am so tempted to just stick it in you and fuck you furiously until I cum deep inside you as you lie there unable to move. But I know that as spent as you are, I can still get another climax or two out of you.

© Martin Toye

To be continued…

THE SCENT OF POSSIBILITIES

samarelart.com

He thought he saw something in her eyes
Something he needed to see
Although he saw what wasn't there
It became his reality

Looking through his eyes, he saw beauty unparalleled
The eyes of winter fire, the curve of breast and shoulder
The perfect nose, the length of neck, the swell of calf
Formed a perfect melody, the symphony of his desire

Looking through his mind, he saw intellect unbound
The ideal word, the flawless thought, the unspoiled rumination
The language of the artist, sculpting reflections of loveliness
Formed a perfect concerto, the opus of his passion

Looking through his heart, he saw possibilities previously unknown
The dream of tenderness, the dream of feeling, of the solitude of togetherness
The delicate glance, the unintentional brush of flesh, the quickened breath
Formed the final masterpiece, the harmony of his soul

The scent of possibilities had always been there for him
He breathed her in and reveled in her bouquet
The aroma breathtaking, the perfume overpowering
The fragrant apple that enticed forbidden attraction

He thought he saw something in her eyes
Something he desired to see
But passion will alter sight and desire will blind
And force the fantasy of what is not there or could ever be

After dancing out of control without ever taking the lead
The realization came upon him that what he saw was but a
dream
At her request, he slows their frantic dance to a pleasing
melody
And found that this new dance also brought joy and peace

So the dance progressed more smoothly
Each movement no longer carefully planned
Each partner now at ease with the other
They move as one, in perfect harmony.

But suddenly the music quickens and he falls out of step
The scent of possibilities, once the perfume of his dreams
Has once again weakened his sensibilities

Is it possible the possibilities considered are no longer his alone?

Should he advance on his perception that perhaps she feels the same?
What could it mean, she's enticed, she surrenders?
In tune with deeper desires? His heart pounds in anticipation.
But what if he's misunderstood?

He's torn between his natural desire to take her in his arms
It could be that is what she wants, a quenching for this fire
Perhaps she is only telling him she likes this new dance better
No push, no pull, no trying to convince, given up on leading

He's always used words to try and take her where she could not go
Now it is her words that take him where he is afraid to go
Because he must have read them wrong, her surrender must not be to love
Her desires are deeper, enticed by the scent, but not by the touch

Could it be that what was once only possible in his mind
Has begun to creep into her heart?
Will they sing their song together or forever be apart?

OUR PLACE IN THE SUN

I am still wallowing in visions of your beauty this morning, fantasy girl. My cock is so hard for you right now. I wish you were here to stroke it up and down with your beautiful hands, to tease the head with your tongue, to take it into your mouth and wrap your lips tightly around it, to slide it into your beautiful, wet, tight pussy and wrap your legs tightly around me, arching your back to meet me as it slides hard in and out of you. God, I want you!

I am imagining you sunbathing, stretched out on your belly in the hot sun. I stand in the shadows and watch you lying there, watch you reach behind you and undo your top to bare your back to the sun, watch you adjust your thong and slide your hands slowly and softly across the cheeks of your ass, lingering there for just a moment. Perhaps you know I am watching. I move out of the shadows and walk toward you. I stand over you, my shadow cast across your face. Your eyes are closed but you know I am there. I bend to pick up the bottle of tanning lotion that is lying there and squeeze a generous portion into my hand. With your top undone, I can see your breast peeking out from underneath where you are lying on it and my cock stirs once again.

My hand slides softly across your back and you give a slight sigh. I begin to rub the lotion into your back, working your muscles gently in the process. My hands glide over your shoulders and down the length of your arms and back up again. I slide my hands down your back and move them down your sides, briefly touching the sides of your perfect breasts. My hands arrive at the curve of your hips and slide across the line of your thong. I gently finger the smooth white peach fuzz on your back, just above your bikini line.

The sun is baking you and there is a beautiful layer of sweat covering your body. It glistens on the cheeks of your ass, enticing me. As I move down to your legs, my hands move across it and you give another brief sigh. I take more lotion into my hands and work it into your legs, starting at your ankles and moving slowly up your calves. When I reach your knees, I travel back down to your ankles, take your feet into my hands and massage the lotion into them. With my thumbs, I massage the balls of your feet and slide a finger slowly and gently between each toe. Your sigh becomes a bit deeper. The smell of the lotion is strong in the air and mixes with the sweet smell of your perspiration as the sun continues to heat your skin. The combination of the scents and the feel of your skin are a powerful stimulant and I can now feel my cock straining against the fabric of my shorts. After relaxing every muscle in your feet, my hands move back up and continue to work the lotion into your legs. Over your calves, to your knees, up the back of your thighs and over the cheeks of your ass, massaging all the while. Your ass is so perfect, I cannot help myself and I spend several minutes massaging those tight muscles. A single moan escapes your throat.

I slide my hands back down to the inside of your thighs and move them back and forth from just below your ass to your knee and back again. With each pass, my hand moves closer to the tiny patch of cloth covering your mound. You part your legs a little further as if begging me to move higher up your thigh. Your breathing has become visibly heavy and you arch your back, sticking your ass further up in the air and giving me better access to the opening of your thighs. Finally, on my upward stroke, the edge of my thumb glances against the cloth of your thong and you gasp and give a small shiver. I can see a touch of moisture in the center of the cloth and know that you want to be touched. My hands slide back up over your ass and grip the top of your thong. You raise your ass slightly to accommodate and I slide your thong down over your cheeks, down your smooth legs and over your feet. My hands begin their climb back up your legs, only this time I do not stop at your thighs. Instead, I slide one finger over your moist slit. Again you gasp and I begin to move my finger back and forth over your delicious, moist pussy. Your clit begins to swell at my touch and your breathing grows heavier. You arch your back and push your ass up into the air as an invitation to my finger. I accept and slide one finger into your wet pussy. You moan loudly and begin to move your ass up and down, shoving my finger deeper and deeper inside you. You reach underneath you with one hand and place a fingertip against your clit and begin to rub it while my finger presses into you. I watch you rub your clit while my finger slides in and out and it is such an incredible turn-on.

My cock is ready to explode and I can stand it no longer. I pull off my shorts and climb over you, your finger moving frantically against your clit. You raise your ass higher and I place the head of my cock against your slit and slide the head of it back and forth over your pussy, soaking it in your wetness. You are breathing heavy and desperately rubbing yourself. As your finger moves back and forth over your clit, I can feel the tip of it touching the head of my cock. I am so hard for you! I hear you say under your breath, "fuck me...fuck me NOW!" You push your pussy up against the head of my cock and the head slides inside you.

The heat from your pussy is almost unbearable and you are so wet and ready that my cock slides all the way into you on the first thrust. This time, it is my turn to moan. I begin to move in and out of you and the feel of your perfect ass against my belly is the most erotic thing I have ever felt. I know that I will not last long, but you are continuing to rub urgently at

your clit and I can tell you are almost there. My cock is
pounding in and out of you and you are slamming your ass
against me, rocking violently. I feel a wave starting in the pit
of my stomach and know I will not make it another stroke.

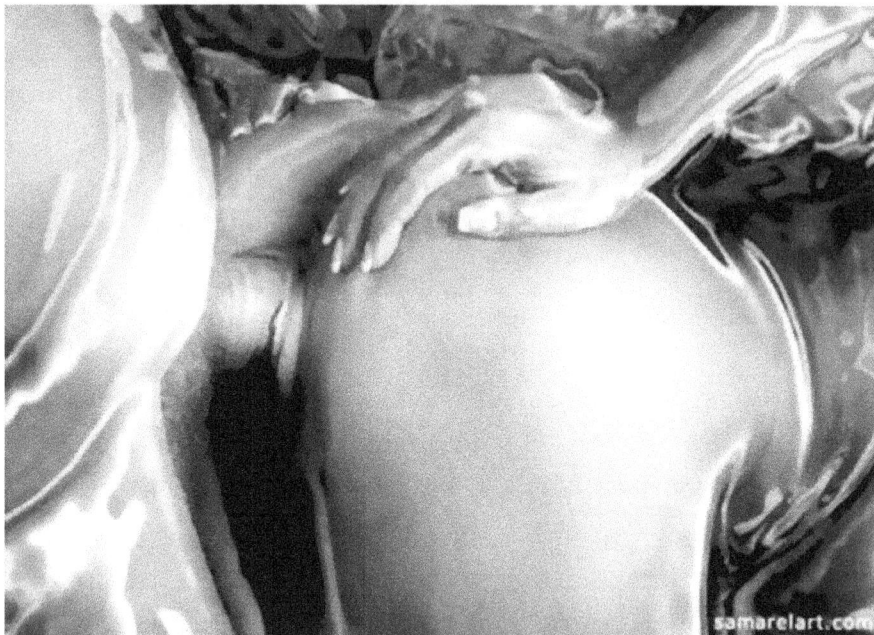

At that moment, I feel the muscles of your pussy grip me
tightly and begin to convulse around my cock. You are
bucking wildly and begin to scream, which instantly carries
me over the top. With your ass beating against my belly, your
pussy gripping me tightly and your shouts of ecstasy exciting
me as I've never been before, I explode deep inside you. The
waves wash over me and it feels as though it will never end. I
continue to move in and out of you as we cum hard and
long. After an eternity, we collapse together on the ground,
unable to move. I lay there with you, breathe you in and
don't ever want to exhale.

Thank you for a lovely dream, fantasy girl. Can you make this
real for me?

ONLY A FANTASY

samarelart.com

This offering is a rape fantasy, because so many requested it. It is not a violent rape fantasy, really more of a bondage tale, and its intent is strictly role playing between two people in a loving relationship. Rape is a horrifying and heinous crime that could never be condoned by this writer. If any of you have been a victim of this terrible crime, I ask that you please not read it. The last thing that I would ever want is to cause pain over it. Go read "Cum to Vegas" again, or perhaps "Mass Transit". Fantasy girl's masturbation story is a really good one, too.

You arrive home from work, weary from your long day. You swing the door open and walk through, but before you can close the door, you are grabbed from behind, a hand clasped over your mouth. You give a sharp gasp, your body tenses and your heart begins to race. You feel the hot breath in your ear and the whisper, "don't scream". You stand there, your mind racing with thoughts of what you should do. The hand is tight and is holding your head back, but begins to relax slightly against your mouth. There is an arm wrapped around your torso, holding you firmly. The arm moves and you feel a hand moving across your belly. It slides under your blouse and is now hot against the flesh of your stomach. You feel the hot breath against your neck and the breathing gets heavier as the hand rubs circles slowly on your belly. The hand over your mouth pulls your head back further and you involuntarily move backwards until your back and ass are tight against the body behind you. You feel the hand move from your belly upwards and begin to massage your breast through your bra. The breath against your neck becomes more of a pant and you feel a growing pressure as something begins to grow against the curve of your ass. The hand massaging your breast grabs the top of your bra and yanks it down, baring your breast to the touch of the silk of your blouse. The hand returns to your breast and begins to pinch your nipple. You breathe in sharply. You don't want it to happen, but your nipple begins to swell and you feel a twinge in your sex.

You feel lips against your neck, sucking at you, the hand moving back and forth between your tits, squeezing them hard and pinching at your nipples. A tongue runs up the side of your neck to your ear and you feel teeth nipping at your earlobe. The hand moves from your tits back down your belly to the waistline of your skirt. It lingers there for a moment, then one finger slides below the waistline and you feel the hand beginning to work its way into your panties. You try to block it out, but when that first finger reaches your clit, you can feel that it is already swollen and moist. The finger begins to manipulate you, tracing circles on your clit and your breathing becomes heavier. You don't mean to do it, but you find that you are moving your ass against the bulge that is now poking hard against you. You feel teeth on your shoulder as the pressure on your clit becomes almost unbearable. The finger is rotating faster and faster and harder and harder against you and you can't help but respond. The hand over your mouth is making it difficult for you to breathe and you find that you are actually panting. Suddenly, a finger slides deep inside you. You press your ass back against the pressure poking into your back and begin rocking your hips to the rhythm of the finger sliding in and out of you, its base resting firmly against and grinding into your clit with each plunge of the finger. Your stomach muscles clench tightly, you arch your back and push your ass harder into the raging cock stabbing you from behind. The muscles of your pussy grip the finger tightly and your juices are released over it as the first wave hits you. You cum long and hard, your pussy convulsing at the power of your orgasm. Your knees become weak and if it weren't for the hand holding back your head and the arm wrapped around you with its hand between your thighs, you would collapse to the floor.

The finger is still rotating slowly inside you and you are feeling the final spasms of your climax when you hear softly in your ear, "I'm going to move my hand...stay quiet". The pressure over your mouth begins to relax and the finger slides out of you, making you gasp again. The hand slides out of your panties and you begin to turn your head to see what's behind you. A hand grabs your hair and the sharp whisper returns..."don't turn around".

You realize your body is still pressed back hard against the resistance and you begin to relax when suddenly hands appear at each side of your face and a scarf is placed over your eyes. It is tied tight over your face, but it is not uncomfortable. For a moment, you are disoriented, but quickly recover. You start to ask a question, but the hand moves back over your mouth and you understand.

As you stand there, you feel a hand against your thigh. It moves up under your skirt and begins to squeeze your ass. After a moment, it moves from under your skirt and up to your hip and you can feel that your skirt is being removed. You feel it slide down your legs and drop to the floor. With a violent wrench, your panties are ripped from your body and again, you gasp. A hand on your arm turns you to face your stranger. Now, you feel the buttons on your blouse being undone, slowly, one at a time. You feel cool air caress your tender nipples and you know your blouse is now hanging open. It is pulled from your shoulders and drops to the floor. An arm circles your waist and pulls you in tight. The still hard cock is pressed into your belly as the hand moves up your back and with one quick movement, unhooks your bra. Like your skirt and blouse before it, your bra falls to the floor and you are standing there naked.

The hand slides down your back and again grips your ass, kneading it roughly. The arm releases you and you move your arm to cover your breasts and move your other hand over

your mound. But you feel a tight grip on your wrists pulling
your arms away from your body, and resigned, you lower
them to your side. You stand there silently for a long time.
There is no sound except for the steady exhale of heavy
breath. You can feel eyes burning into your flesh, traveling
up and down your body. Again, you feel a strange excitement
starting to build.

After an eternity, you feel a hand on your arm and you are
being guided blindfolded through the house. You can tell
from your route that you are headed for the bedroom. When
you reach it, the hand turns you once again to face your
stranger. A hand lightly on your chest, between your breasts,
gently pushes you backwards until the edge of the bed is
against the back of your knees. A final light push and you fall
back onto the bed. You want to resist but instead, find
yourself pulling yourself back to the center of the bed. You
hear the drawer of your nightstand open and close. You feel
a hand on your wrist followed by the feel of silk and you
realize your arm is being tied with one of the silk scarves from
the drawer. You begin to struggle, but suddenly feel a
tremendous weight on your chest, knocking the air and any
fight out of you. The weight is removed and you catch your
breath. You lie there quietly and feel the silk being placed
around your other arm and then each of your legs as you are
tied spread-eagled to the four corners of the bed. You are
completely and utterly exposed, but instead of
embarrassment, you feel a tense thrill.

You can actually feel the eyes on your body. Down your long
neck to your breasts where you feel the tingle in your nipples
as eyes burn into them and cause them to pucker. You find
yourself tightening your stomach muscles, hoping to draw
that hot stare, now craving the lust that you know your
perfect body is inducing. You find that the eyes drinking in
your naked flesh is causing warmth in your sex again and you

begin to move your body slightly from side to side and arch your back, almost as if in a seductive dance. You hear footsteps leaving the room and realize you have been left alone. You struggle a bit just to test your bindings and quickly realize that you cannot escape.

The footsteps return and with each step, you hear a tinkling that you can't identify. Something is set down on the nightstand. You hear rustling and then the sound of a zipper and you know what is coming next. Suddenly, the weight is back on your chest, but it is no longer heavy. You feel something fleshy and burning hot rubbing against your nipples and again, you feel them begin to swell. The weight shifts, moving higher on your chest and you jump with surprise as this heat is pressed against your lips. You jerk your head to the side, but hands on the sides of your face position your head upright. Again, you feel the heat and pressure against your lips and you part them to release your tongue. For a moment you consider biting down hard, but as if your thoughts are being read, you feel a hand grab a handful of your hair and you give it a second thought. Besides, the feel of the smooth, hot flesh against your lips has given you that throb in your sex and warmth in your belly and now you only want to explore. Your tongue flicks out and begins to glide over the head of the cock. You explore it hungrily, circling your tongue over the head, running it up and down the long shaft, exploring the glans.

samarelart.com

The weight on top of you shifts again and you feel a hand behind your neck, holding your head up and the head of the cock slips into your mouth. You suck on it greedily, working it hard to try and pull some sound, a moan, a sigh, anything from your stranger. But nothing. Total silence. You become all the more determined and as you suck on the head, your tongue runs circles around it. You feel the cock begin to inch its way deeper and begins to move in and out gripped tightly by your lips. With each stroke it moves deeper into you and soon you are fucking it hard with your mouth. You take it all, devouring every inch. You can feel the cock beginning to swell and know that within seconds, hot cum will shoot down your throat. A smile of satisfaction crosses your face as you realize you are about to conquer the stranger and you can feel your own clit stiffen at the thought of milking his soul through his cock, when suddenly a hand on your forehead pushes your head away and the cock is pulled from your lips. You are left there panting and aching and squirming. There is a whisper in your ear. "Not yet...I'm a long way from being through with you".

You feel the silk being removed from your ankles. Your legs are lifted and a forearm behind your knees forces them to bend. Your knees are pressed against your chest, forcing your ass into the air. You know the cock will soon be splitting you open, but you are ready. Your pussy is hot and wet. There is no sound and no movement. The forearm is still pressed behind your knees, but not putting pressure on you, simply holding you in place. You hear it before you ever feel it. A sharp whap followed by a tingling in your ass cheek. You shout out, but more from surprise than from pain. Now you know what is happening and you feel an odd rush. Again, a hand slaps your ass hard and you gasp and feel the burn. Now your other cheek. Back and forth, the hand burns your ass cheeks and with each stroke, you gasp. With each strike, you find that you are becoming more and more turned on.

You can feel your pussy getting wetter and wetter. The hand begins moving closer and closer to center and as the circle becomes smaller, the swats become less violent. Your gasp turns into a moan as the first swat meets your clit. There is little strength behind the slaps now, but it is still strong enough, still enflaming. The slaps continue against your clit and you push against the arm holding your legs, but it remains firm. Your clit is swelling and each slap sends an electric jolt through you. The arm holding you down moves away, but you no longer want it to stop. You keep your knees up and your ass in the air and just as you feel like your clit will explode from the spanking, you feel two fingers slide deep into your pussy just as the hand strikes your clit. Your passion overflows and you scream out in ecstasy. This time, no hand rushes to cover your mouth and you scream out over and over again as you cum so hard you can't breathe and each strike against your clit and each plunge of the fingers deep into your pussy only increase the intensity of your orgasm. The crashing of your climax becomes so strong, you can no longer scream. Your head is thrown back and your mouth is wide open, but no sound can come out. After several moments of non-stop heaving and cumming and bucking and cumming and lurching and cumming, you collapse in a heap, gasping for breath.

You feel the fingers slide slowly out of you. The heat on your ass and pussy is so intense. You hear the tinkling again but cannot even think straight enough to wonder what it is. You find out soon enough as the ice cube is pressed against your clit and you scream out in shock. Your surprise is instantly replaced by pleasure as the ice immediately pulls the heat from your burning clit, soothing it and exciting it at the same time. The ice moves slowly in circles around your clit, water tickling you as it runs down your ass and again you begin to move your hips in rhythm with the movement. You begin to feel a warmth building again, in spite of the ice, but the hand suddenly moves away from your clit and you feel the ice trailing up over your mound and onto your belly. As it circles your belly, ice water pools in your belly button. The ice continues to travel upward and your back arches again from its chill. It reaches your breast and traces the swell under each breast, first the right and then moving to your left. It moves in a slowly narrowing circle around your breast until at last it reaches your nipple, which is already swollen from desire.

At the moment the ice touches you, you feel burning heat against your clit once again, which causes yet another jolt through you. It feels so good but you can't figure out why your clit is throbbing again. The ice against your nipple and the heat against your clit have you disoriented. But as the heat becomes pressure and the pressure becomes movement, you realize that the heat is from a tongue massaging your clit. Again, you find your hips rocking to the movement. You don't notice that the ice is no longer circling your nipple. You try to force your pussy harder against this tongue that is giving you so much pleasure, but your bound wrists are keeping you from sliding down any further. You long to grind against your stranger's face, but can't get any leverage. Instead, you are teased with light flicking, making you insane with need. You beg for release and as if in answer, you feel a finger slide inside you. But that's not what makes you scream out. It is the ice, transferred to mouth and now being forced against your clit by the tongue. The movement of the tongue and the shock of the ice have you as hard and swollen as a cherry pit. You feel your third orgasm starting to build, but suddenly all motion, all touch, every sensation ceases. You are left there gasping. You kick out with your legs and scream out "you son-of-a-bitch, finish me NOW!"

You feel hands tight around your ankles and your legs are forced up and once again you find your knees against your chest. With no warning, you feel the head of a cock part your lips and you feel it plunge all the way deep inside your dripping wet pussy. It feels as if it will split you apart, but it is such a delicious pain. You feel the crooks of arms behind your knees, keeping you pinned down and forcing your ass and pussy high into the air. At this angle, the cock is finding every inch of your burning pussy and you feel it going deeper inside you than any cock has every reached. There is nothing gentle, nothing passionate, nothing love-making about it. You are being fucked and fucked hard.

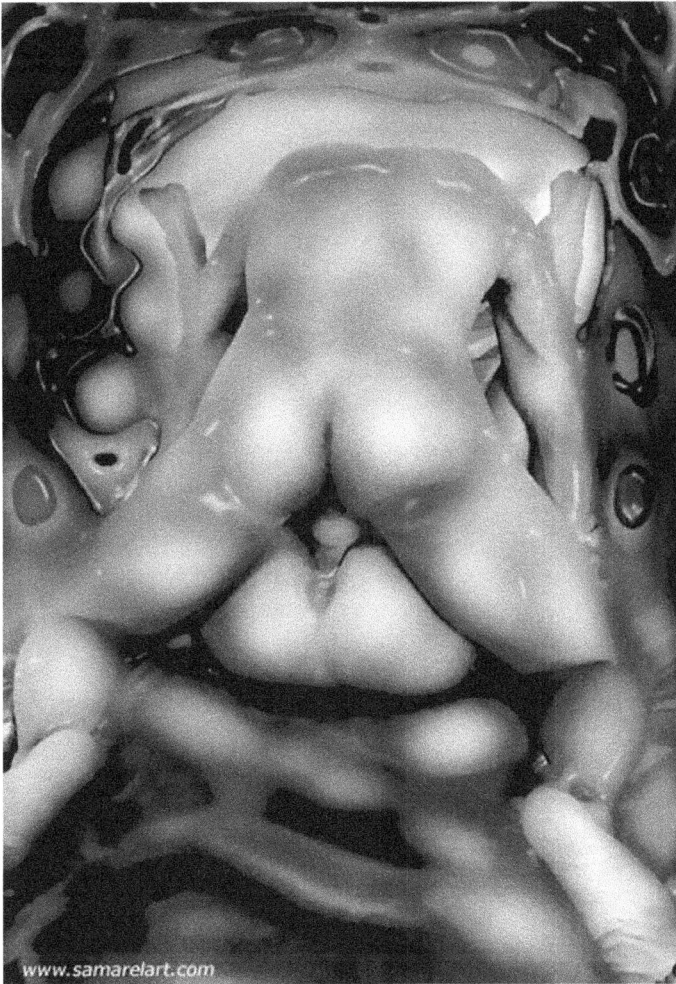

www.samarelart.com

The cock is slamming in and out of you, hitting bottom, stretching the walls of your pussy, the shaft grinding against your clit with every pounding stroke. Never have you been fucked so hard and never has it felt so incredible. Your ass is gyrating, your back arching and you grind your clit against the base of this cock pounding into you. A heat begins to build deep inside your pussy and you rock harder, trying to drive the cock even deeper inside you. The cock moves faster and faster and you are rocking harder against it, driving it in and out, in and out.

A moan begins in your throat, breaks from your lips and turns into a scream as the first wave hits you. As you cum, the walls of your pussy spasm around the pounding cock. As your pussy grips it tighter and tighter, you feel it swell instantly and explode inside you, causing you to cum even more strongly. You begin to shudder as your climax takes over every part of your body. Your pussy continues to convulse in raging orgasm. The cock is still slamming into your pussy and your screams become deafening as wave after wave rolls over you. You can't stop cumming, nor do you ever want to. You feel your legs released and you lower them and wrap them tight around the strangers back, grinding your heels into his upper thighs. You force your clit tight against him and gyrate your hips as the waves continue to crash. Another wave moves up through your belly to your chest and out to your tits and you feel your climax explode through your nipples. With one last scream, you watch the fireworks exploding on the inside of your blindfold, your body gives one last violent spasm and then collapses, completely spent.

As you lie there gasping, you feel the cock being pulled from you, the shifting of weight, and the untying of one wrist. You hear the rustle of clothing being scooped up and the sound of bare feet walking away. You manage to gather enough breath to gasp "who are you", but silence is your only response.

THREE

Hello, fantasy girl. I haven't been able to stop thinking about you, as always. I've been remembering the story you told me about you and your girlfriend. If I close my eyes, I can see the two of you here before me.

I see you sitting close together on the couch. I watch as you lean forward and touch your lips to hers, first briefly and then lingering. You part your lips slightly and your tongue shoots out playfully and touches her lips. She opens her mouth to accept you and I watch as your tongues move back and forth against each other, slowly, seductively. You feel a tingle in your pussy as you imagine her soft tongue against your clit and you can tell she is feeling the same as she moves closer to you, your tongues entwined. You put your hand on the back of her head and pull her in closer, now kissing her deeply. She responds by pressing her body against you and wraps her arms around you, pulling you tightly against her. You begin kissing more passionately, your tongues moving rapidly now. You slide your tongue into her mouth and she sucks it, sweetly pulling it in and out of her mouth. Watching the two of you has my cock so hard and I begin to slide my hand up and down its shaft through my pants.

As your kisses become more passionate, you move your hand to her breast and begin to knead it through her top, pinching her nipple lightly between your fingers. She responds with a low moan and reaches for your breast also. You feel her hands on you, squeezing your perfect breasts, tugging at your nipples, her tongue buried deep in your mouth. You can feel the dampness beginning to grow in your panties and as you squirm at her touch, the fabric of your panties rubs against your clit, getting you so hot. She moves her hand under your top and the warmth of her hand against your bare breast is heaven. She squeezes your nipples lightly and you begin to breathe heavier, fully aroused by her touch. She pulls your top over your head exposing your breasts and bends down and slides her tongue over them. She teases you with her tongue, tracing circles around your nipple, but not quite touching it. You are getting so hot, you can't help but slide your hand down under your skirt and begin rubbing your clit through your panties. Watching this, I open my fly and pull out my member. You glance over at me and smile as I begin to stroke my cock in rhythm with your finger on your clit.

Suddenly, she throws her leg over you and straddles your thigh. Her mouth is back on yours and you kiss deeply and urgently. She pulls her top off and shoves her nipple into your mouth and you suck at it greedily. She presses tightly against your leg and begins to slide her pussy back and forth on your thigh, her nipple still in your mouth. You nip at it with your teeth and squeeze her breast with your hand, loving the feel of her wet pussy rubbing against your thigh. You reach down and place one hand on each cheek of her ass and begin to pull her back and forth on you, grinding your thigh against her pussy. You can feel her heat and how wet she is for you. Her arms are wrapped tight around your neck and she begins to moan as she rides you. You can tell she is about to cum and you reach around behind her ass and press the tip of your finger against her slit, moving it back and forth over her pussy as she grinds against you. I watch as she throws back her head and screams, cumming hard against your thigh. You rock her faster and faster, shoving your thigh tight against her clit and suddenly sliding your finger into her pussy, starting her climax all over again. Her entire body spasms as the second orgasm immediately follows the first and finally she collapses and falls back onto the couch.

You stand up over her and slowly remove your clothes as she watches you, the hunger evident in her eyes. You stand naked before her and she reaches out and slides her hand up your thigh. You feel her hand, warm and soft, against your pussy and she slides a finger over your clit, which is already swollen and wet. She moves the tip of her finger back and forth, first slowly and gently, but gradually going faster and harder. As you stand there, she slips one finger inside you and you gasp in pleasure. She moves her finger in and out of you and it feels so good! She slides a second finger into you and you rock back and forth as she finger fucks you. She moves her thumb to your clit and rubs it while her fingers slide inside your tight, wet pussy. You moan as you feel your climax start to build. You grab her hand and pull it from you and straddle her face, lowering your dripping pussy onto her mouth.

You press your clit tightly against her lips and she begins to fuck you with her tongue. Grabbing the top of her head, you grind your clit against her face as her tongue glides in and out of your pussy. She grabs your ass and squeezes your cheeks, fucking your pussy hard with her tongue and you scream out as you cum over her face, your juices flowing into her mouth and down her chin. The waves of ecstasy hit you over and over again as you continue to cum, her tongue deep inside you. As I watch the ecstasy on your face and her tongue in your pussy, my cock is straining to explode and I have to fight back my orgasm, saving my load for you.

You collapse beside her on the couch, your knees weak, your pussy throbbing. She leans toward you and kisses you gently. You can taste your pussy on her lips and you lick your juices from her face. You tell her you want to make her cum again and you slowly move your lips from hers, down to her neck. You bury your face in her neck, sucking and licking at it. Your hand moves to her breast and you squeeze her nipples between your fingers and she begins to respond. I watch as your mouth moves down her neck, across her chest and sucks at her nipples, your hand now on her inner thigh and moving slowly upward toward her hot, wet pussy. As you suck her nipples into your mouth, biting at them with your teeth, she squirms beneath you and her breathing quickens. She breathes in sharply as your fingers finally reach her pussy and you paint circles around her clit with the tip of your middle finger. She arches her back and whispers "fuck me" in your ear. You slip one finger inside her tight pussy and grant her wish, slowly fucking her and sucking at her nipples. As she begins to respond, your tongue slides from her breasts and down her belly. You can smell the sweet smell of her wet pussy and you feel her hands on your head, pushing you towards it. You kiss her lower belly, her hips, her mound, her inner thighs, all the while, your finger sliding in and out of her pussy. At last, your tongue reaches her clit and you flick it lightly, teasing gently.

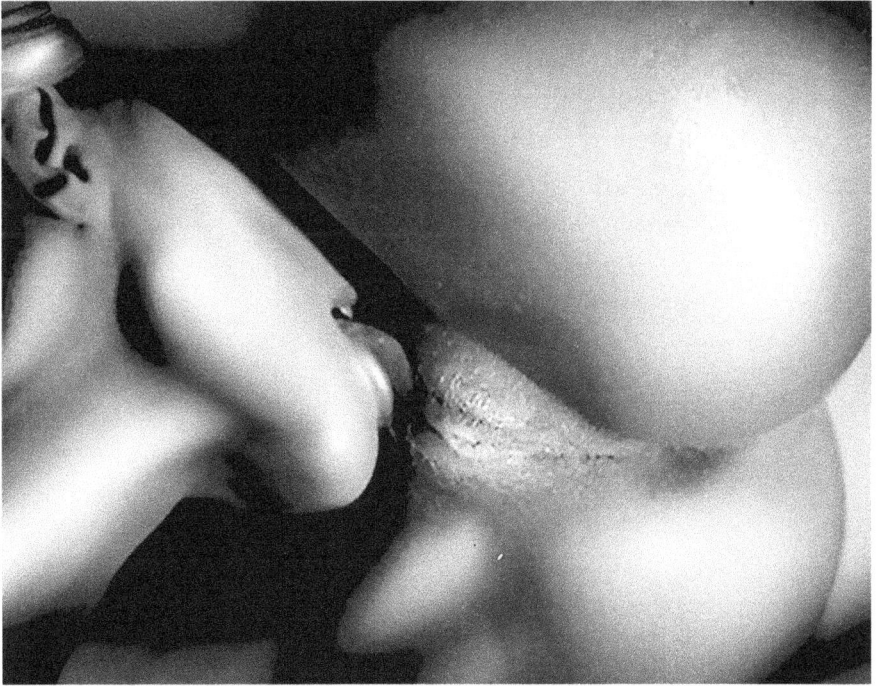

You slide your finger deep inside her and with its tip, you push upward against the inside of her pussy and make small circles against her g-spot. She gasps and bucks convulsively, driving your finger hard against her. You suck her clit into your mouth and circle it with your tongue. She arches her back and grinds against your face, your finger pushing against her g-spot, your tongue pushing against her clit and she explodes. She grips the back of your head hard, pushing into you, twitching uncontrollably. After cumming for an eternity, she collapses, spent and gasping.

This is such an amazing turn-on for me! A dream come true. My only hope is that the two of you still have some left for me. You answer that question for me with a question of your own.

You watch her as she catches her breath and begins to smile. You rise from between her legs and ask, "Would you like some more?" She smiles and nods and you turn around and position yourself on top of her, your head between her legs, hers between yours. You lower yourself until your pussy is directly over her mouth and you breathe in deeply as her tongue reaches out and slides along your clit. You lower your face to her pussy and gently begin to lick and tease at her clit, which is still swollen and hard from cumming. You feel her tongue against your clit and you sigh with pleasure as she begins to move faster against it.

(samarelart.com)

I stand and begin to slip out of my clothes, my cock rock hard and standing straight out. You raise your head from her pussy and say "I want your cock" before returning to her clit. I stand there a while longer and watch the two of you, your faces each buried in the other's pussy, stroking my cock as I look on. I move behind you and watch up close as your ass moves up and down on her face, her tongue against your clit, her hands on your ass, spreading your cheeks as she licks you. It is such a beautiful, perfect sight.

I move my face closer and begin to tongue your ass while she licks your clit. My tongue touches against hers over and over as we both work your pussy and ass with our mouths. I can feel her hot breath against my face as her excitement begins to build from your tongue on her clit. You begin to move your ass back and forth against us, pushing your clit against her tongue, pushing your ass against mine. All the while, I'm stroking my cock, which is now ready to burst.

I rise to my knees and move in close behind you. I place the head of my cock against your clit and feel her hot, wet mouth on me as she makes me wet for you. I push my cock into her mouth and she sucks at it greedily. I pull it out and rub its head against your slit while she moves her tongue against your button and over my shaft. I slide the head inside you and you moan with pleasure. As I push into your tight pussy, I can feel her tongue all along the underside of my cock as she licks both your clit and my shaft at the same time. You begin to moan louder as I begin to slide my cock in and out of you, my hands on your hips, her tongue on your clit, my balls sliding across her forehead, over her eyes, down her nose. She gyrates beneath you as your tongue brings her closer and closer to another climax. You begin to shake, also getting closer, as her tongue continues to press against your clit. I can feel your pussy beginning to tighten around my cock and I can't control it any longer. I begin to fuck your pussy hard, slamming in and out, feeling you clenching me tightly, feeling her tongue sliding up and down my shaft at the same time she is pressing it against your clit. My balls are slapping against the bridge of her nose, my cock is pounding in and out of your pussy, her tongue is pressing against your clit while you eat her fast and hard.

I hear the first scream but don't know who it is coming from. She begins to shake and buck against your tongue, her arms wrapped around your lower back, pulling you tight against her mouth. I can feel your sex clenching tightly around me. The convulsions of your pussy and your screaming tell me that you are cumming hard. The sight of the both of you cumming together and the feel of your hot, tight pussy convulsing around my cock is all I can stand and I explode inside you. My cock is pounding in and out of you, filling you with hot cum as your pussy spasms around me. Her tongue is still tight against you as your orgasm overwhelms you and I can still feel her tongue against my cock as it slides in and out of you. As our orgasms subside and my cock begins to slow inside you, she licks my shaft and your pussy clean, tasting our juices together. Too weak to continue, the three of us collapse together in each others arms.

My love, I would give anything if you would make this happen for me. Please.

TWO FIRES – PART THREE

... You are barely able to move, every muscle in your body completely limp as the fire crackles in the fireplace. But I know that as spent as you are, I can still get another climax or two out of you.

I watch you from between your thighs as you smile in euphoria, completely sated. Again, I blow softly against you, the cool air soothing your red and swollen pussy. I breathe in your intoxicating scent and find my own personal heaven. Experiencing you is the greatest joy I have ever known and I live now only to bring you pleasure. I lay my head against your thigh and pray that you will be with me forever.

You slowly recover from your powerful climax and raise yourself up from the couch. You move to me and begin to kiss me deeply, tasting your juices on my lips and muttering "thank you...thank you...thank you". Your hands are on my chest and you slowly begin to inch them down my body until, once again, you hold my cock tenderly in your velvet hand. You say "your turn..."

Slowly, your lips move down my body, your warm, sensuous hand moving up and down on my fully engorged cock. You kiss down my chest, across my belly and onto my inner thighs, your tongue flicking out against my fevered flesh. You know how ready I am for you and you don't make me wait, replacing your hand with your mouth and licking at my member with your soft tongue.

I move my hand to your cheek and push it back through your hair, smiling as I watch. I watch as you circle the head of my cock with your pink tongue, teasing it as your hand moves up and down on me. Your mouth and hand feel so good. You suck on the head of my cock and continue to stroke me. Slowly, your mouth engulfs me, your lips moving over the head and down my long shaft until you have swallowed my entire cock. I can feel its head in your throat and it causes me to tremble with desire. Your lips move back up my member until they reach the sensitive ridge at its head, then back down until the shaft has completely disappeared into your mouth. Up and down you move, your tongue caressing the underside of my cock with every long stroke, and each time the head passes into your throat, I breathe in sharply. My fingers run through your hair again and find the back of your head and I find myself pulling you down on me, my hips moving in rhythm with your luscious lips, fucking your mouth.

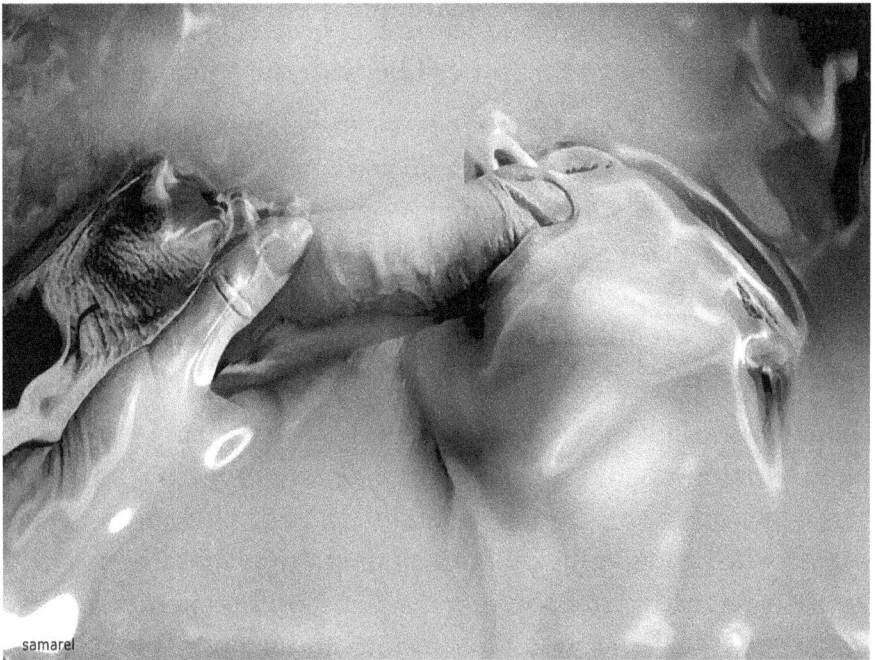

samarel

I feel your hand on my balls, cupping them, kneading them gently as my cock moves in and out of your throat. I move my leg against you and you shift your position to straddle it, your mouth never losing its delicious rhythm on my angry cock. I feel your wetness as you lower yourself onto me and begin to rub your pussy against my leg. I can feel the heat of your desire against my flesh, exciting me, and my need for release grows. Your growing excitement is evident as you suck my organ more urgently and I can feel the beginnings of an incredible climax in the pit of my stomach. You feel my cock swelling in your mouth, my balls tightening in your hand and you know that I will be filling your throat with hot cum in seconds, causing you to grind even harder against me. My leg is slick with your juices and the heat radiating from your pussy is fuel to my fire. You hump my leg wildly and the moans in your throat reverberate through my cock, causing a sensation I've never felt before. I need to cum. I need to cum now.

"I'm gonna cum," I pant, but you stop immediately and climb up over my belly, gasping "no...no...no" and you straddle me. Grabbing my raging cock, precum leaking from its tip, you place it against your drenched pussy and sit down hard on it.

I penetrate you deeply and savagely and you scream out as your earth-shattering orgasm crashes into you. Your pussy pulses around my cock as it plunges in and out of you and I explode, pumping hot cum deep into you as you ride me hard and fast. Your hair hangs in my face as you rock your hips, waves of ecstasy pounding your body, bucking and jerking over me, my cock slamming in and out of your pussy. I cum and cum again, spurting my hot juices into you. You cum and cum again as my cock invades your convulsing pussy violently and frantically.

Our explosive orgasms subside to that muscle-jerking, delicious, just-came sensation in our sexes and you collapse on top of me. Your lips find mine and you slip your tongue into my mouth and kiss me deeply. We lie there together, your breasts pressed to my chest, your lips pressed to mine, the warmth of your pussy comforting around my fading member. And when the final swelling of my cock diminishes and I fall from you, I can't help but feel a longing for more.

To be continued…

TRUST ME

© Steve Anderson Photography

I have a surprise for you, fantasy girl. Do you trust me?

I pull a silk scarf from my pocket and you turn your back to me and I place it gently over your eyes, tying it firmly but not too tightly behind your head. I turn you around to face me and move my lips to yours. The touch startles you and you flinch, but you respond, opening your mouth slightly and touching your tongue to mine. We kiss tenderly and the feel of your soft lips against mine, the tip of your tongue flicking out to meet mine, sends a warmth through my entire body. After several long moments, I reluctantly break our kiss and take you by the hand. "Come with me, my love". The feel of your hand in mine is pure velvet and my thumb caresses the back of your hand as I lead you.

We walk slowly and carefully...you hear the door open and smell fresh air. I guide you slowly down the steps and you hear the car door open...I help you in and close the door. You hear the door on the driver's side open and close and the start of the engine. "Where are you taking me?" My only response is "Do you trust me?"

As I drive, I cannot resist resting my hand on your thigh and I massage it gently, sliding it up beneath your skirt, tickling you with my fingertips. I watch your nervousness subside as a contented smile appears on your lips. You feel the slightest soft touch against your lips and jump in surprise for a second time. But as my finger moves gently over your lips, you figure it out and smile, taking the tip into your mouth and sliding your tongue over the pad, sucking gently. I feel a twinge in my groin and hope that you are feeling the same.

After some time, the car pulls to a stop, you hear the door open and close and footsteps drawing near your door. It opens and I take your hand once again, helping you out of the car. I guide you and we walk together, your hand in mine, your other gripping my arm. You hear the rattle of a doorknob and a door opening. I guide you inside and you listen as the door closes behind us. I take your arm and we begin to move down stairs, moving slowly and carefully. We arrive at the bottom and take just a few steps inside. I turn you to face me and place my lips to yours. What begins as a soft, gentle kiss becomes more passionate as you wrap your arms around my neck and our tongues entwine. My hands reach for your breasts and a shiver goes through you as I massage them through your top, finding your nipples and rubbing them between my thumb and forefinger. You moan softly and your hands wander over my body, over my chest, my back, down to my ass and then sliding around my hip to massage my stiffening cock through my pants. Our kisses grow more urgent, our hands groping and squeezing and stroking each other. As passion grows, my lips move to your neck and I suck gently at your flesh, flicking my tongue out to taste your flesh, nipping softly at you with my teeth.

I step back from you and begin to slowly undress you, unbuttoning your blouse and sliding it over your shoulders, unbuttoning your skirt and watching it fall to the floor, unhooking your bra and releasing your beautiful, perfect breasts. I can't resist them and cup them in my hands, massaging them gently. I move my lips to them and feel a shudder run through your body as I take each nipple into my mouth, tenderly circling them with my tongue until they are firm and swollen. You feel the charge all the way through you. You feel a surge of warmth in your sex and a tingle runs through your clit. With my tongue still circling your nipples, I slide my hands down your back, under your panties and pull them down over your ass to your thighs. They slide slowly down your legs to the floor. Feeling them pooled around your ankles, you step out of them and stand naked before me.

We separate and I stand back and look at you, marveling at your perfect body. You feel my eyes burning into you...you feel their heat against your long neck, against your firm breasts, tickling your perfect belly, sliding over your hips. But mostly, you can feel them on the flesh of your sex. You squirm as the sensation warms you and your hands begin to move absentmindedly over your body, cupping your breasts, caressing your belly, sliding over your ass, moving down between your legs. You are not surprised to find that your pussy is wet with desire. Nor are you surprised when you feel me take your hand and raise it to my mouth, moving the tip of my tongue over your fingers, tasting your musk.

You feel me take your other hand in mine as well. I move them together so that I am holding both of your hands in one of mine. I whisper into your ear "Do you trust me?" and you feel cold steel against your wrist and hear the snap of a metal clasp...and then again on your other wrist.

© Jean-Paul Four

You gasp and struggle against the restraint, but I take you into my arms and hold you tight to my chest, whispering softly in your ear. My words seem to calm you and you stand before me, shaking nervously. I begin moving my hands over your body, massaging your breasts again, taking your ass into my hands, sliding my hand with a glancing touch between your legs. I bury my face in your neck and my lips and tongue begin to savor you as my hands wander your body. I can feel your body relaxing and your tenseness is soon replaced by want. You sigh gently as my hands and lips move over you. Desire begins to build and is soon sweeping through your body, causing your breasts to swell, your nipples to tingle, your clit to pulse in time with your beating heart. You feel my hand move between your legs and tickle softly over your sex and you moan as my fingers whisper over your lips.

Again, "Do you trust me?" in your ear. Something yanks at the metal around your wrists and you hear the rattle of chains. Suddenly, the whine of a motor and your hands are being pulled over your head. You jerk in surprise and holler out, "What the fuck is going on?!" but there is no response.

Your arms are pulled higher and higher over your head, dragged by the restraints around your wrists. You rise up onto your tiptoes to relieve the growing pressure in your wrists when suddenly the pulling stops. Again you holler "WHAT THE FUCK IS GOING ON?!" Again, no response. You shift from foot to beautiful foot, high up on your toes, trying to lessen your weight against the restraints that are holding you almost off the ground. "LET ME DOWN!" But there is nothing but silence. You kick out with one leg, finding only empty air, causing you to lose your footing and you swing back and forth until you can get your feet under you once again. For several minutes, you hang there helplessly, blindfolded, naked, exposed, vulnerable. You listen intently, but can hear no sound.

There is a faint sound...perhaps a leather against leather kind of sound. You can't quite make out what it is, when suddenly, WHAP! You feel something slap hard across your ass and you yell out "OWWW", more from shock than anything. Before you can recover, WHAP! again across your bare ass. Now, you can feel the burn, a fire on the flesh of your backside and you are surprised to find that it is exciting you. Your pussy is pulsing in anticipation of the next stroke and your breathing is ragged. WHAP! It strikes again, raising red welts on your ass and you scream out, this time from pleasure. WHAP! WHAP! WHAP! You cry out, your pussy now dripping, your tits swollen and sensitive. "HARDER" you cry and before the word has died in the air, WHAP!, your wish is granted. You press your thighs tightly together and begin to work them against each other, trying hard to stimulate your engorged clit. WHAP! The pain is intense and you begin to weep, tears running down your cheeks. WHAP! One of the leather straps finds its way between your legs and strikes directly on your clit and you scream out. The pain is overwhelming, the pleasure even more so. You spread your legs as far as your tiptoes will allow you to, arching your back and pushing out your ass...WHAP! Another strike hard across your ass. "MY PUSSY! MY PUSSY! HIT MY FUCKING PUSSY!" Before the words are out of your mouth, WHAP!, several straps snap against your swollen and enraged sex. You scream out, "FUCK!!!" WHAP! WHAP! WHAP!, each strike finding your dripping pussy. You shout out "DON"T STOP!" and lift one leg high off the ground, fully exposing your slit. WHAP! WHAP! You scream out as your body explodes in orgasm WHAP! each strike bringing with it a fresh, pounding wave. WHAP! Tears pour down your face and your screams are relentless as your overpowering orgasm racks your body WHAP! Each strap of leather against your blazing pussy bringing with it its own intense pain and incredibly delicious pleasure. WHAP! WHAP! It is as if each stroke starts your climax anew and you cum WHAP! and cum WHAP! and cum. You collapse, dangling from your restraints, sobbing and whimpering, "please stop, please stop, stop, you fuck."

Your pussy is on fire, red and swollen, yet you still feel the reminder of your earth-shattering orgasm as your heartbeat pounds in your clit, throbbing and pulsating. As the fire on your ass and the throbbing in your pussy begin to subside, you begin to feel the pain in your wrists and armpits as you hang. You try to regain your feet, but you are too weak, your orgasm too powerful. You feel hands at your hips, pulling you up, taking the pressure off your arms and wrists and you collapse against me, your head on my shoulder. You feel nuzzling against your neck and shoulder and a tingle begins anew in your swollen sex. Your sobs abate and a slight smile crosses your lips. You bury your face in my shoulder, wallowing tenderly in our closeness. You raise your head and kiss my face, searching for my lips. You find them and kiss me deeply. You breathe into my ear, "That was amazing," and seek out my lips again, slipping your tongue into my mouth, taking mine into yours. You kiss me hungrily and rub your body against mine. My hands are on your ass, holding you up, taking the weight off your wrists, and you wrap your legs tightly around me. Our kisses become more fevered, sucking at each other's tongues and you grind against my body. I can feel your excitement beginning to build again as you rock your hips against me.

You feel my hands grip your ass and lift you. In your darkness behind the blindfold, you are disoriented, as your body is lifted higher and higher. My hands move from your ass to the back of your thighs and your legs are raised up and over my shoulders. You are lowered down onto my shoulders in a reverse piggyback and I breathe in your scent, sweet and pungent from your multiple orgasms. Your aroma is incredibly intoxicating, enflaming me and without ceremony, I bury my face in your pussy. My tongue finds your clit and you moan loudly as I lap at your slit, slipping the tip into you, sliding up and down over your wetness, drawing circles in the pink flesh surrounding your button.

Raised off the ground as you are, you reach up and grab the chain that suspends you, pulling yourself up and rocking your hips into my face, grinding your pussy into my mouth.

samarelart.com

I pull your engorged clit into my mouth and suck hard at it, pulling it into my mouth, squeezing and pinching it between my lips. You buck against my face, your moans growing louder. I grip your clit tightly between my lips and pull on it, stretching it out from your body while the tip of my tongue presses against your rock hard button. You feel the waves beginning again in your belly and press furiously against my face, using the leverage of your legs on my shoulders to slam your pussy into me. Your climax begins to build and a scream starts in your chest. Just as it moves into your throat, I slide my hand under your ass and plunge my thumb into your dripping pussy and an instant later, you feel a wet finger push into your ass. You scream long and loud, grinding into my face, feeling every powerful sensation at once...my mouth sucking hard at your clit, my thumb pounding your enflamed pussy, my finger plunging in and out of your ass. Your body begins to jerk and shudder uncontrollably on my shoulders as wave after wave of overpowering orgasm pounds every nerve in your body. Your pussy slams into my face over and over as you cum violently, your body convulsing as spasm after orgasmic spasm rocks you. After long moments of screaming, cumming, bucking, grinding, you collapse over me, drained of strength, unable to hold yourself up any longer.

I grab you under your arms and lift you off my shoulders. Through your daze, you hear the whine of electric motor again and your feet settle flat on the floor, the pressure taken off your wrists and arms. It stops though with your arms still above your head, but you are no longer hanging from them. You lie against my chest until you can regain your strength and are able to stand on your own feet again. You feel me pull away from you, listening to my footsteps as I move away and then return. You feel my hands around your thin ankles, you feel my fingers moving over your beautiful feet, rubbing them gently. You feel my lips against them, my tongue touching softly, then slipping between your toes.

You recognize the feel of leather being wrapped around your ankle and realize instantly what is happening. You kick out your leg at me, but I grab it and wrap my arm tightly around your calf, holding your leg still as I finish buckling the restraint around your ankle. You whimper, "No more, sweetheart, no more", but I continue. You give up your struggle and I place the leather shackle around your other ankle.

You hear the motor again and your arms are released. You feel me removing the chain from between your wrists, but you are still cuffed. You hear me say, "Spread your legs", and you do it, but the restraint between your ankles stops you just beyond shoulder-width.

Suddenly, you are yanked forward by the cuffs, bent over double, almost losing your balance. You hear and feel me rustling between your ankles and when it stops, you can't move your wrists, you can't stand up…your hands have been shackled to the ankle restraint. You are bent over double and restrained so you cannot move.

You are surprised to find an ache growing in your sex. You hear something slide across the floor, and suddenly there is a table in front of you. You feel me push your head down and it finds the softness of a pillow and you lay your head on the table, your legs apart, your ass in the air, your pussy exposed.

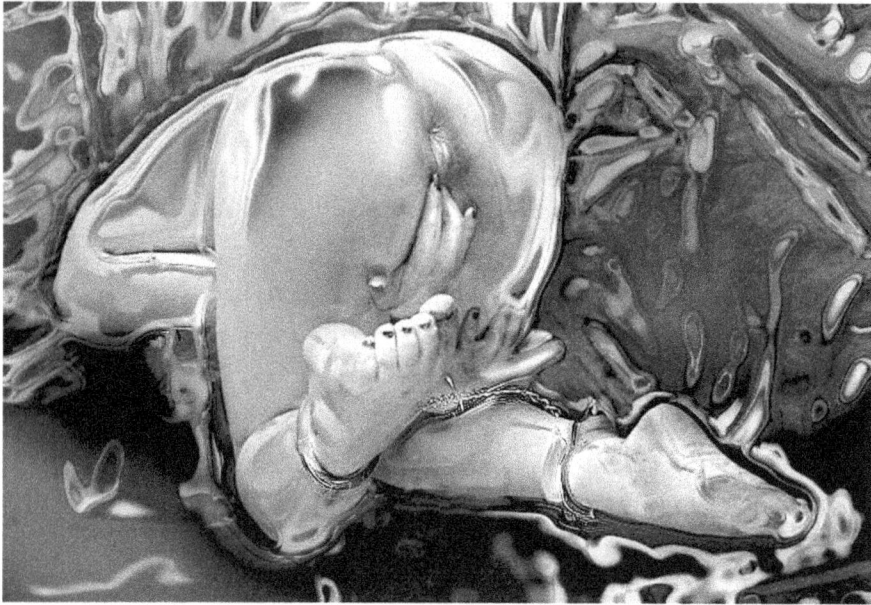

You can sense me standing behind you. A light breeze blows across your pussy, soothing you, relieving the heat from your burning flesh. My cool breath begins to warm you and you find yourself becoming aroused. My hands flow gently over your red and swollen ass, increasing your want. They move to your legs and glide softly up and down, tickling your inner thighs, and you sigh with pleasure. "I want your cock..." Instead you feel the soft, velvety touch of my tongue against your pussy, gently licking you. I spread your cheeks, move my lips to your ass and begin to tongue you there, running the tip around your rim. Back and forth from your pussy to your ass, slippery and smooth. I linger at your clit and enjoy feeling it swell and listening to your moans. I slip my tongue inside your pussy and move back and forth, fucking you slowly with my tongue. I move to your ass and push the tip into you and begin to work my way slowly into you until I'm buried all the way inside you. Again you are moaning, again you are moving your hips, searching out my tongue, your desire to be fucked growing stronger. You struggle against your bonds, trying to regain control, but you are held tight.

You feel me step up behind you. The heat from the head of my cock is intense against your sex. You feel the tip moving up and down on your pussy, parting your lips, teasing your clit, slipping just past your opening, circling you endlessly. "Stick it in me...fuck me now," but it continues to tease, driving you into a frenzy. You try to push your hips back against me, but it only makes you lose your balance. All you can do is arch your back and beg. Your pussy is dripping wet...you are so ready to be fucked. And I am so ready to fuck you. I step closer to you and you feel my belly against your ass, my cock between your legs, sliding back and forth over your lips, drenching my cock in your juices.

You feel my hands on your tits, squeezing them and pinching your nipples, sending shivers up your back. You rock your hips back and forth, trying to find the head of my cock with your pussy, needing to feel me inside you. Suddenly, you feel a sharp pain at your nipple, followed by incredible pleasure shooting through your tits and you recognize the feel of the nipple clamp, first at one tit, then the other. You moan louder and writhe with desire. The pain is intense and you savor it for the pleasure that comes with it. You move your ass back and forth, searching for my cock, begging to be fucked. Your pussy throbs, both from the abuse it has taken and in anticipation of the hard fucking you are about to get. I won't make you wait any longer.

Stepping up behind you, I take my cock in my hand and place the head of it against your slit. With one hard shove, my cock is buried deep in your pussy. You scream out, the thrust of my cock splitting you in half. The pleasure is exquisite as I begin to move back and forth, in and out of your pussy. You struggle, trying to take control of our fucking, but you can't, the restraints holding you firmly in place. My hands are on your hips and I plunge into you, making you cry out in ecstasy, my cock filling you completely.

You bend over as far as the restraints and table will allow, shoving your ass out and trying to get my cock further into you and I oblige, pounding it in until it is not possible to fuck you any deeper, stretching you to your limits. The pleasure is so intense, you pant and gasp for breath.

Your head bangs into the pillow over and over as I slam into you, my cock finding your g-spot, causing you to squeal uncontrollably. "Pinch my clit!" you holler and I reach around you and squeeze it tightly between my fingers. With my other hand, I reach around and grab the chain attached to your nipple clamps and tug at it. Again you scream out at the overwhelming pain/pleasure that racks your body. "FUCK ME!!" you scream, followed by "make me cum, you fuck!" I pound my cock into you, hard and fast, and roll your clit between my thumb and finger. "Oh fuck, I'm cumming!" you scream out. As my cock slams furiously into you, your orgasm does the same, knocking you from your feet, leaving you lying over the table, jerking and shuddering. Your body is thrashing involuntarily as you cum violently, wave after wave after wave smashing into you. You lose all control as the powerful sensations rock you, taking you over, slamming into every nerve. Your juices flood my cock and flow freely over my balls and down your thighs. The clenching and convulsing of your burning, soaked pussy around my plunging cock is more than I can stand and I explode into you, filling you to overflowing with my hot cum. The intensity forces me to collapse onto your back, my cock still pumping your aching sex, my cum still squirting into your throbbing pussy. You grip me tightly, squeezing every drop of cum from me.

We lie there for a moment, gasping for breath, weak and drained. Gradually, you feel me rise from you. The clamps are removed from your ultra-sensitive nipples, causing a shiver to run through you. You feel me at your ankles and your arms are suddenly free. You feel me undoing the buckles that bind your ankles and finally the rasp of metal as the cuffs are removed from your wrists. You turn to face me and our lips find each other again. You kiss me deep and hard. I hear under your breath, "thank you thank you thank you."

My hands are behind your head, untying your blindfold. As it falls, you look around and smile at the block and tackle extending from the ceiling, the wall of restraints, the handcuffs built into the wall. You turn to me..."You just drove me around the block?? I love what you've done with my basement."

AT YOUR FEET

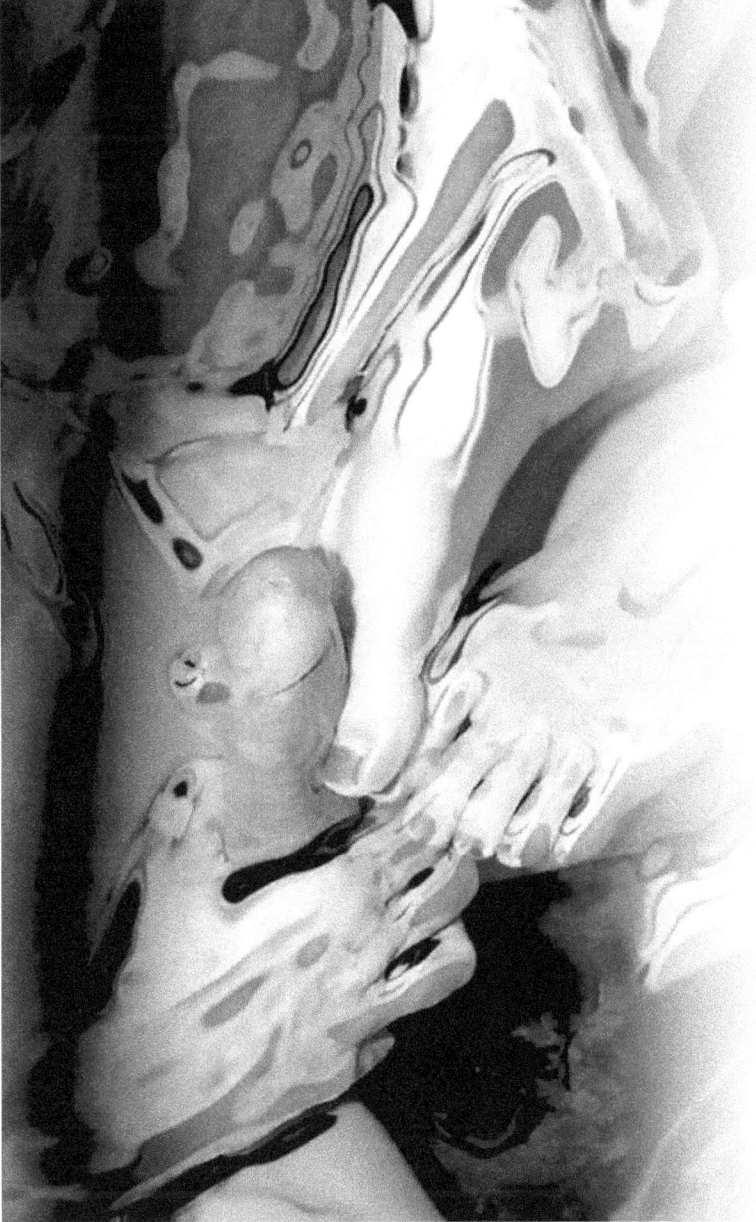

Massaging your feet has always been one of my favorite things to do, fantasy girl. And I know how much you love it as well. But tonight, you took me so by surprise. So unexpected and so incredible.

As you always are, you were with me on the couch, me sitting at one end, you lying at the other, your feet in my lap. You have the most adorable feet and I love caressing them as you lie there. With my fingers wrapped around them, I use my thumbs to massage the ball of your foot, pressing hard enough to relieve the stress of being in heels all day. My thumbs slide over the bottoms of your feet, down to your heel where I press into your flesh, working all of the tension out of your feet. Taking each toe individually between thumb and finger and massaging the pad. But my favorite part is sliding a finger gently between your toes and watching your face as your eyes close and that faint smile creeps across your lips. It never fails to quicken your breathing and mine always follows.

But tonight was different. Rising from your position, you instructed me to lie down and you moved to the far end, sitting on the arm with your feet up on the couch. You sat there watching me from the opposite end of the couch, never saying a word, your eyes just traveling up and down my body. My eyes were glued to your beautiful feet and recognizing the look on my face, you taunted me by stretching out your legs over my body and wiggling your toes, spreading them wide, clenching them like a fist, drawing circles in the air. I watched fascinated. You put a foot on each of my knees and began to slowly move them up my thighs, stopping just short of my groin. "Take off your pants", you instructed and of course, I always obey. I lie back down on the couch, my excitement beginning to show in anticipation of what is to come.

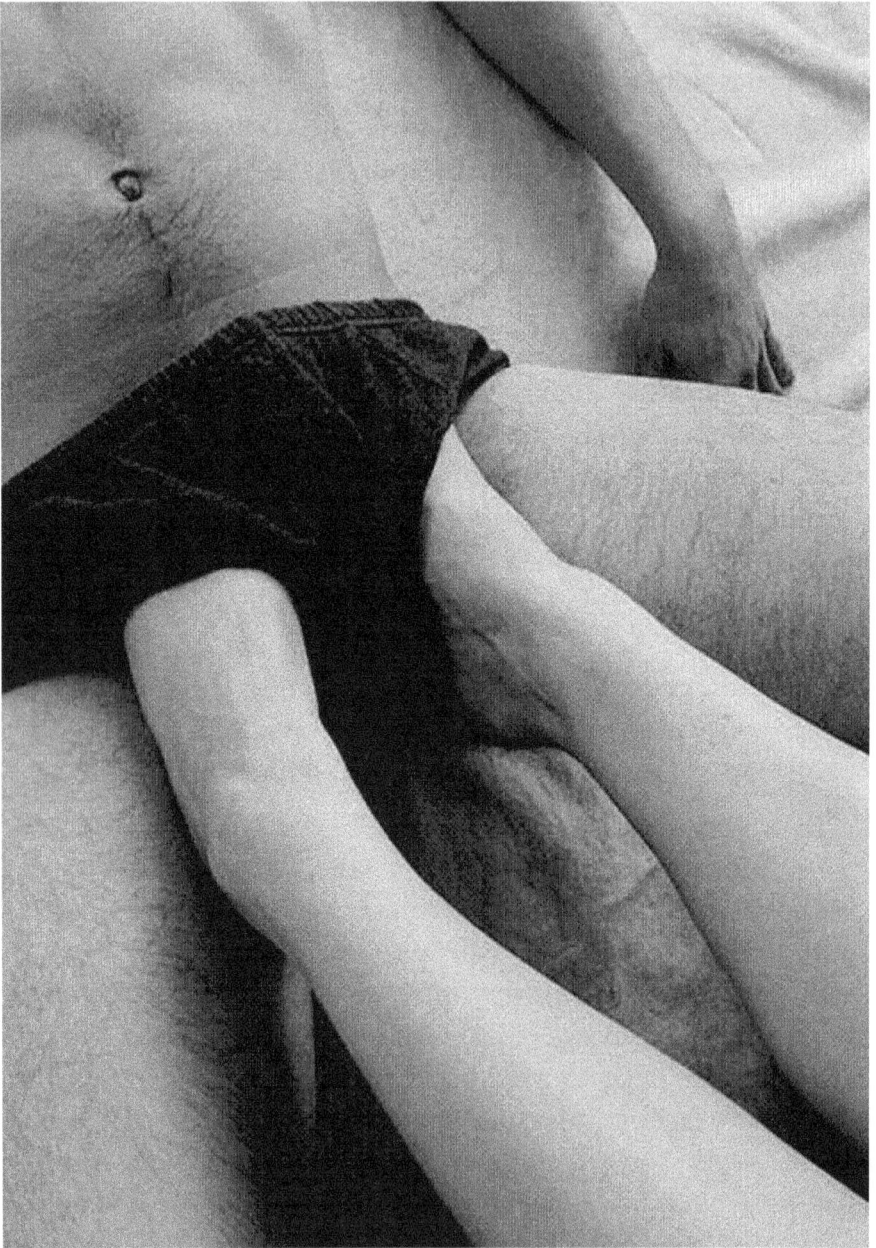

Sliding your feet back up my legs, you tease at my inner thighs for a bit with your toes, and then you slide one foot beneath my crotch and begin to wiggle your toes, massaging my balls gently. As my cock began to grow, you moved your foot up over my balls to its base and slid your toes slowly up and down its shaft. Almost immediately, my cock grew to its full height and you began to use both feet, stroking it up and down between the balls of your feet. You held it upright with one foot while massaging it up and down with the toes of your other foot. You slid your toes over the head of my cock, tickling the tip and rubbing over the top.

After a few minutes of teasing my cock with your toes, you asked me to lie on the floor beside the couch. You moved to the center of the couch and placed your feet on my belly. My cock was standing straight up, totally aroused. With your right foot, you massaged my chest and with your left, oh your incredible left, you placed your instep against the underside of my cock and pushed it down onto my belly, trapping it between your foot and my stomach. You began to slide your foot up and down on my cock, from my balls up to that ultra-sensitive spot at the ridge of my head. It was the most amazing feeling! You would roll the head of my cock under the full length of your foot and then return to stroking it up and down. I couldn't take my eyes off of your feet working my body, but with a furtive glance, I could see that your hand was moving rapidly between your legs. After only a few minutes of you pressing my cock into my stomach and stroking it up and down, I could feel the familiar twinge in the pit of my stomach and knew it wouldn't be long before I exploded all over my chest and your feet. I could tell that you were getting close as well as you rubbed your pussy frantically, causing your foot to move faster and faster on my cock, bringing me ever closer.

Although I would have loved to have you finish me with your feet and now wish I had, experiencing that pleasure for the first time, I wanted to bring you pleasure as well. Rising, I pulled you from your seat, dragged you to the end of the couch and shoved you back over the arm. Your shoulders pressed into the cushions with your ass high up on the arm, just the right height for me to enter you. Without ceremony, I did, pressing the head of my cock into your pussy and pushing into you. As I begin to move inside you, you placed your feet flat against my chest and with one hand, I caressed them while the other gripped your thigh and pulled you toward me as I fucked you.

My cock pumped in and out of you, my ass working like a piston, driving you into the cushions. Your moans grew louder and you reached out and grabbed the arm of the couch at each side of your ass, pulling hard on it and bucking your hips, slamming your pussy into me. You slid your feet up my chest, over my neck and to my face, raising your ass higher and forcing my cock deeper into you, your moans becoming growls. With a sole on each cheek, I wallowed in your feet, kissing them, sliding them over my face, slipping my tongue between your toes. My cock plunged hard into you and your ass slapped against my thighs. The growl in your chest began to rise into your throat and you fucked me furiously, my cock slamming into you, my face buried in your feet. Just as the growl broke free of your throat, I took a toe into my mouth and sucked hard on it and you screamed out as your orgasm found you and you took me with you.

It was a hard, gasping orgasm for the both of us. Your body shuddering and thrashing on the couch as I convulsed over you, continuing to suck at your toes as I exploded inside you. You threw your head back, your mouth open wide, but no sound came forth as your body quivered and shook, wave after delicious wave crashing over you. I could feel my orgasm in every nerve of my body, so intense, my entire body spasming over you. As the force of my climax subsided, I slid from you and lie on the floor next to the couch. As I lie there panting and attempting to catch my breath, once again I felt the soft flesh of your feet caressing me and I reached out to take them in my hands.

Fantasy girl, there is nothing sexier than a well formed foot and yours are so very well formed. I think there is a good chance that you have turned my love of your feet into a fetish!

HARD AT WORK

You know what you are doing to me. You tease me, your words taunting me, knowing the effect they are having on me. I know you are sitting there grinning like crazy, knowing how much you are making me want you. Well, you're right. I do want you. Here. Now. I close my eyes and I can see you before me. Reaching under my desk, my fingertips trace the outline of my engorged cock through the material of my pants. Yes, there you are, behind my eyelids. Come to me...

There is a noise at my door that startles me from my fantasy and I open my eyes. You are standing in my doorway, posed perfectly, one hand on your hip, a sly smile on your face. My eyes are drawn to your gorgeous breasts, straining against the silk of your pale blue blouse. You say, "Need any help?" and step inside. You move slowly and seductively toward me. You step around my desk, reach down and take the arms of my chair in your hands and push me back from my desk. My cock is straining against my pants, my hand frozen on it from the shock of seeing you standing there.

"Oooooo...for me?" and you bend over and take my hand away and replace it with yours. Lowering my fly, you reach inside and release my throbbing member, teasing its head, tickling my balls, and then softly and slowly stroking me up and down. Your touch is heaven and my cock grows even harder, every vein engorged, bright blue. Just when I think I can't possibly get harder, with your free hand, you lift your long black skirt and my heart pounds in my chest to see that you aren't wearing any panties. Your lips are pink and slightly swollen with that perfect narrow crease between them and I can't help but wish I was parting them with my tongue.

While you continue to tease my cock with the lightest of touches, I reach out and slowly undo the buttons of your blouse, exposing your perfect breasts, hidden from me by the white lace of your bra. Pinching the clasp between your breasts and giving a slight squeeze, I release the clasp. The white lace falls open and your beautiful breasts are there before me, inches from my face. Leaning forward, I kiss them, caressing them with my lips, my tongue flicking out to taste your flesh. Taking a nipple into my mouth, I pinch it gently between my lips and feel it stiffen. My hands move to your legs behind your knees and I slide your skirt up, my fingers caressing the backs of your legs as they move higher. I move from nipple to nipple, sucking, nipping at them with my teeth, as my hands continue upward until they are cupping your ass. All the while, you are stroking my cock gently. I massage your ass with one hand while the other slides around your thigh and I seek and find your pussy with the tip of my finger. I part your lips with my finger and move it slowly back and forth over your clit, barely touching, feeling it beginning to swell. As it grows, I draw tiny circles around it, your dampness turning into wetness, making my finger slick. You begin to sigh softly, your clit now fully aroused and I move my finger to your slit and begin my circles on your opening, pressing a bit harder until the tip of my finger is inside you, still drawing circles and inching slowly into your drenched pussy. I'm trying so hard to concentrate on pleasing you to distract me from your hand moving up and down on my cock, trying so hard not to cum just yet. My finger is now buried deep inside you, exploring every tiny bit of you, searching for that wonderful little ridge deep inside your pussy, that little ball of flesh, knowing that when I find it, I can take you over the top. Ahh, there it is...

Your sighs turn to moans and you take a step back from me, releasing my cock and pulling from my finger. I can see the want in your eyes and you can see the need in mine. Standing before me with your blouse hanging open, your beautiful breasts at my eye level, you grab the hem of your skirt and pull it up over your waist. You spread your legs and straddle me, lowering yourself onto my lap. I cannot take my eyes from you, nor do I ever want to. I lean back in my chair and my cock strains upward toward your pussy. You reach down between your legs, take my cock in your hand and rub the head of it over your slit, using it to part your wet lips. You slide tip back and forth between your lips, spreading them further and further and then slowly lower yourself onto me and the tip of my cock enters you. You ease down onto my lap, my hands on your hips pulling you down, my cock slowly inching its way deep into your pussy. The velvet smoothness of your sex wrapped around my cock, its heat, its wetness, makes me shudder with pleasure and the length and thickness of my member does the same for you. A moan escapes our throats simultaneously.

You place your hands on my shoulders and begin to raise and lower yourself onto my cock. My hands grip your hips more tightly as the pleasure overtakes me and I begin to pull you up and down more urgently. Leaning back in my chair, I have such a perfect view of you and I watch, completely hypnotized by my cock sliding in and out of your pussy. You lean back, improving my view and you fuck me long and hard, my eyes glued to you.

Loose strands of hair fall about your face and stick to your neck. Reaching out, I remove the tie from your hair and it falls down your back, flying wildly about as you fuck me furiously. I entwine my fingers in your hair and pull your head back, burying my face in your neck. You feel my cock splitting your lips, their flesh pulled in and out by my thrusts.

As my excitement grows, I move my hands to your tits, kneading and pulling and squeezing and pinching at your nipples. You begin to move faster over me, bouncing hard on my cock and it pounds in and out of you, thick and hard, filling every bit of you. I push my ass up off my chair, driving my cock even deeper inside you. The head of my cock finds your g-spot and you gasp in pleasure. You begin moving faster and harder, my cock slamming into you, hitting your spot with every stroke. I move my hands back to your ass again, grabbing and squeezing it hard, yanking you up and down faster and faster on my enraged cock.

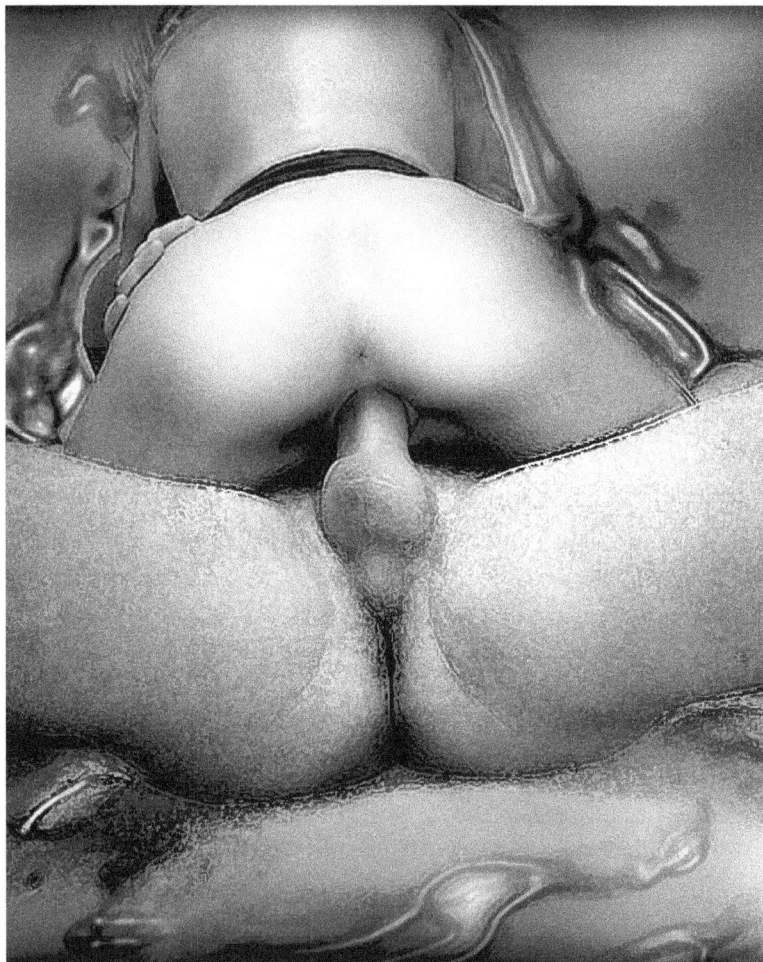

Your moans grow louder and louder, my cock pounding into you. Your climax slams into you and you scream out. My ass is bouncing up off the chair as my cock stabs into you harder and harder and the force of your orgasm causes your entire body to spasm against me.

I suddenly stand up, lifting you off the floor, driving my cock even deeper into you. Again you scream out, the waves of ecstasy washing over you. With one arm, I clear my desk, spin you around and throw you down on it, my cock hammering in and out of you.

With one hand wrapped in your hair, I hold you down and with my other, I reach around you and find your clit with my fingers. You are panting and moaning and screaming as you continue to cum in multiple orgasms that will not stop. My cock is slamming into you, your ass is slapping against my thighs, your orgasm overwhelming. With each pounding stroke of my cock, your orgasm intensifies until your entire body is jerking and convulsing on my desk and there is one long continuous scream coming from your throat. Your pussy is clenching and pulsing around me so tightly, your clit throbbing and pulsating, your juices soaking me. Leaning over on top of you, holding you down hard on the desk, my cock jack-hammering in and out of you, I can stand it no longer and I explode deep inside you. You can feel every spurt of my hot cum pumping into you, and your orgasm reaches a new peak, your body shaking and shuddering beneath me, our juices overflowing. I collapse on top of you, both of us panting and gasping, too weak to move. We stay there for many long minutes, feeling my cock gradually subside until it is completely limp, but still inside you.

Your heat and your wetness feel so wonderful around my soft cock. Can I stay here for awhile?

Opening my eyes at last, I'm saddened that it was all just a dream. I am alone, without my fantasy girl.

TABLE FOR TWO

I am watching you right now, standing in my kitchen, bent at the waist and leaning over the counter. Your legs are spread and your skirt is pulled up and as I sit here on my couch, you are teasing me with your perfect ass and beautiful, moist pussy. God, I am soooo dying to slide my tongue into you, to taste your delicious juices, to breathe in your heavenly scent, to fuck you with my tongue. I was tempted to sit here and stroke my cock while I watch you, but you have a way of bringing me to my knees.

Your ass is so perfect it makes my head reel...do you mind if I wallow in it a bit? I want to bury my face in it, cover every inch of it with my lips, followed closely by my tongue. I want to press my cheeks to it...massage my entire face with it. But that can only lead to me tonguing your asshole. Would you like to feel my tongue flirting with your pink hole? I'm spreading your cheeks with my hands, squeezing and kneading them as my tongue works around the edges of your sweet opening. Can you feel the tip of my tongue beginning to work its way inside you, slowly, gently? Can you feel the tip flicking in and out of you?

I want to taste you deeply...my tongue is working its way into you, moving in a little deeper with each push...pulling slowly out and pushing back in, a little further this time... can you feel my tongue stretching you? Will you rub your clit for me while my tongue burrows into your ass? Make it swell for me, sweetie. My tongue is buried all the way inside you...feel the tip exploring the walls, drawing circles inside your ass. It's moving so much easier in and out of you now. God, I love your ass! I love how tight it is around my tongue, I love how you rock your hips back and forth, helping me to fuck you, I love how your cheeks press against mine as my tongue slides in and out of you. Would you like me to fuck you faster? Can you take me a little deeper? I have a little bit of tongue that hasn't been inside you yet. Rub your clit a little harder for me. I love sliding my tongue as deep into your ass as it will go, pulling it all the way out to toy with the rim and then plunging it all the way back inside you. My cock is so jealous...it longs to be buried in your tight ass as well, fucking you deep and hard. But that's for another day.

I'm pulling out because there is something else that I want tonight...something I've been longing for forever. Can I kneel here for a bit and watch you touch yourself first though? That gets me so hot! My cock gets enormous just thinking about it. I can't imagine what would happen to it if I could watch it instead of just imagining it. Can we find out...do you mind? Don't make yourself cum though, sweetheart. When your juices flow, I want them to be over my chin. Oh, that looks so good...do it slowly for me, baby. Do you mind if I take my cock out while you do that? I want to stroke it while I watch. Is that okay?

I can't take it any more...I *have* to taste you! I don't want your fingers to have all the fun! Let me tongue your ass again. I want to taste one of my favorite spots...that beautiful, sensitive little stretch of flesh between your ass and your pussy. I linger there for just a moment, kissing it and flicking my tongue out against it. But your scent is drawing me and I can't wait another moment to taste your sweet juices. My tongue moves slowly along the length of your slit, moving upwards toward your engorged clit. God, you taste so good! I love this angle. It is so perfect for eating your pussy...my tongue can so easily part your lips, circle your clit, slip deep into you. Oh sweetie, your clit is so ripe and swollen! Let me tickle it for a bit with the tip of my tongue. Does that feel good? Would you like me to press a little harder? Would you like my tongue flat against you, licking you up and down, or do you just want the tip, drawing circles around your clit? I think just the tip for now, moving through the folds of your pussy, parting your lips, pressing against your tender button. Can you feel me? Can you feel my tongue running up and down on you?

Okay, sweetie, no more teasing...I want to hear you cum. I want your juices to flow into my throat and run down my chin. Arch your back for me...push your pussy up...I want to fuck you with my tongue. Can you feel the tip pressing against your sweetest of openings? Can you feel it enter your pussy? Can you feel it sliding inside you? Push your ass back against my face. No, HARD! Hit me in the face with your ass as my tongue plunges into you.

Feel my hand smack your ass...feel the sting of my hand and the thickness of my tongue buried deep inside you. I can go deeper...let me spread your cheeks a little further. Can you feel my tongue pounding in and out of your hot, throbbing pussy? Slam my face with your ass...harder...faster...fuck my tongue. Fuck it...fuck it harder...

Take this finger up your ass as you ride my tongue. Rub your clit for me now...rub it hard. My tongue is thrusting furiously into you, pounding relentlessly in and out while my finger slams your tight asshole. Do you want two fingers in your ass? Take them deep...rock your hips and take my fingers all the way into your ass. Push your pussy onto my tongue...fuck my tongue... fuck me... ram your slit into my face... keep fucking me... harder... harder... HARDER! Cum for me... cover my face in your cum... cum for me NOW!

Fantasy girl, I have never wanted to fuck anyone as badly as I want to fuck you.

THE RAILING

Hello again, fantasy girl. I'm missing you badly, sitting here in my hotel room. Standing out on my balcony, I had a vision of you. This one is really brief, but I thought I would share it with you anyway. I like a quickie once and a while too, you know!

I am in my room and hear a noise out on the balcony that overlooks the pool. I go to the window and see a woman standing there with her back to me, leaning over the railing and watching the people in the pool below. Her hair cascades down her back, past the tie of her bikini top. Her skin is bronzed and radiates with a beautiful glow that is accentuated even more by the florescence of her hair across it. She is wearing a tiny little white skirt that barely covers her gorgeous ass and when she leans over to get a better view of the people below, it rides up just enough to show that perfect spot where her legs meet her ass. The heels on her feet give her calves beautiful form and her legs are long and lean and incredibly sexy. Her legs are slightly spread, her knees are straight, her back is arched, all making her ass stick out directly at me. I stand there for a few minutes, just watching her and taking in her perfection. It is my fantasy girl and I find my hand moving toward the rising bulge in my swim trunks and I begin to massage my growing cock through the fabric.

As quietly as possible, I slide back the sliding glass door and step out onto the balcony. I'm standing directly behind you, six stories above the scores of people in and around the pool. Many of them must be looking up at you...no man can be that close to such intense beauty and not stare. I can smell the scent of your body. No longer able to resist the long, sexy expanse of skin, I slide one hand very lightly along your inner thigh. You give a jump and I can hear a sharp gasp from your lips, but you don't turn around. My hand slides from the back of your leg, just below your perfect ass across your inner thigh between your legs and around to the front of your leg. I give your thigh muscle a brief and gentle squeeze and pull my hand back across your inner thigh. I slowly move it up and down your inner thigh, almost to your knee and back, close to the patch of pink panty that is barely covering your most beautiful mound. With each upstroke, I come closer and closer to rubbing my thumb against your panties, but remain a hair's breadth away. You respond by spreading your legs slightly and arching your back a bit further. You never give me more than the back of your head, nor do you take your eyes off the people at the pool.

Again, I slide my hand up your inner thigh and this time, my thumb briefly touches against your panties and I feel heat there. I trace my thumb lightly along the edge of your panties and follow the line up to your ass. Now, with both hands, I cup your cheeks underneath your skirt. You stick your ass out a bit more and I begin to work them with my fingers and palms. I spread your cheeks and release, spread and release, causing your panties to rub against your slit and now your breathing is audible. Your response tells me you are ready for more. I slide one finger under the line of your panty and move it slowly across your slit to your clit. I hear your sharp intake of breath and begin to work your clit with the tip of my finger, feeling it swell against my touch. You lean further over the railing and spread your legs a bit further, giving me better access to your wet pussy. I move my finger more rapidly over your clit and it is now as firm and round as a marble. I pull my finger back just slightly, slide it into your pussy and begin to move it in and out. You begin to rock your hips in rhythm to my finger fucking you and your breathing is now heavy. You never turn your head, but I can sense that your eyes are now closed.

My cock is rock hard. With one hand, I pull my trunks down just far enough to release it while my other hand is busy with two fingers inside you now. You are moaning softly and moving your ass back and forth to meet my fingers, your legs spread wide and your ass protruding. With one hand, I pull your panties to the side and place the head of my cock against your hot, wet pussy. Before I can guide it in, you shove your ass back and my cock buries itself inside you in one quick stroke. Now, it is my turn to gasp. I begin to move my cock in and out of you, sliding all the way out and then all the way back deep into you.

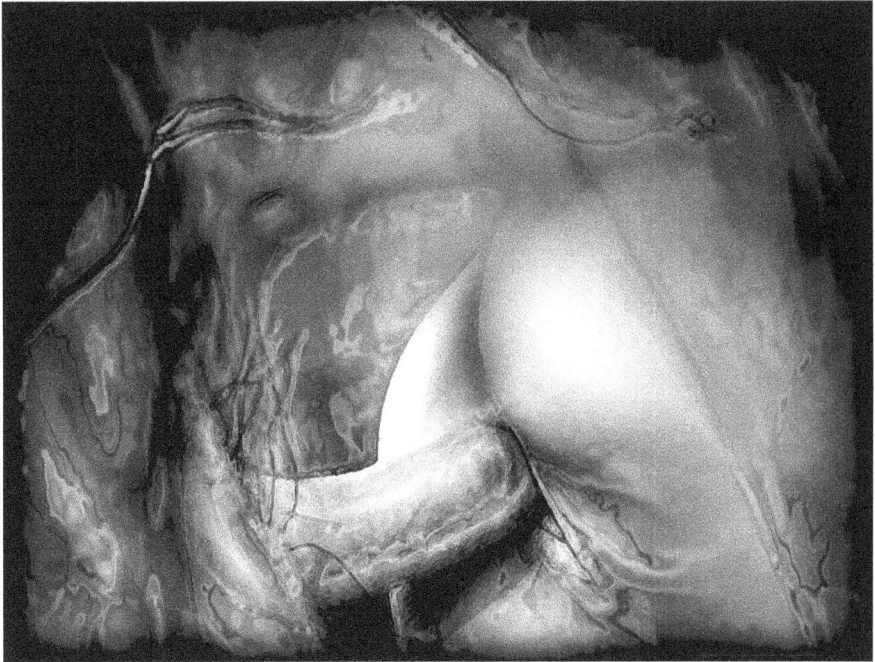

I reach my arms around you and take your breasts into my hands, sliding underneath your bikini top. I squeeze your tits and pinch your nipples as my cock moves faster and faster inside you. At this angle, your pussy is so tight and its muscles grip me so hard, I know I cannot possible last more than a few seconds. But I am passed the point of no return and choose not to fight it back. I can tell you are close anyway so I take my hands from your tits, grab hold of your hips and begin pounding my cock into you. I hear the beginnings of a growl and realize it is coming from my own throat. I briefly notice that people below are now looking up at us, but we are both oblivious to it as my cock slides faster and faster and harder and harder in and out of your incredibly tight pussy. I can feel my climax building in the pit of my stomach and my balls begin to tighten. I watch as you suddenly grip the railing tightly, throw your head back and arch your back further than it is intended to go. I grip your hips tightly and slam my cock into you. You fight back your scream but your pussy begins to spasm around my cock and the intensity of your orgasm takes me over the top and I shoot deep inside you. The convulsions of your pussy as you cum only make me pump you harder and the throbbing of my cock as it shoots brings yet another wave over you. Your climax is so intense that your knees buckle and you collapse over the rail. My cock falls out of you and it is then that we notice that everyone below is watching. I pull up my trunks quickly and walk back through the doorway. I turn back to you, but you are gone.

At least I hope it was you.

THE ROAD TO HEAVEN

© Martin Toye

Hello, my beautiful fantasy girl. I'm going into serious Vegas withdrawals and thought maybe you'd like to come with me this time. I always drive when I go, although it would be much more convenient to fly. It's about a four hour drive, three hours of it on a long, straight, flat stretch of Interstate 15 where you can really open it up. For some reason, driving that stretch of road always makes me horny! It's the perfect stretch of road to cum on.

You are sitting next to me, looking radiant as always, dressed in a tiny little skirt and a top that ends right below your perfect breasts. The top is down and the wind is blowing through your hair. (Okay, so I don't drive a convertible. It's my fantasy and I'm entitled to some poetic license!) The sun is warm on our faces as we speed across the desert. I find that I can't stop looking over at you, marveling at your beauty, made hungry by your bare legs and your bare belly. You notice me looking and with an evil little grin, you kick off your sandals and put your feet up on the dash. Knowing how I love your feet, you taunt me by massaging the dash slowly and seductively with your toes. Your hands move to your knees and you slowly slide them over your legs, down to your ankles, back up to your thighs and back down again, all the while watching my face with mischievous eyes and a seductive smile. You move your feet further apart on the dash and begin to move your knees slowly together and then wide apart, again and again, causing your skirt to ride high up on your thighs and I can see the curve of your ass. My cock begins to swell as my eyes travel up and down your legs, from your cute little toes up to the curve of your perfect ass.

You reach down and recline the seat, just a little bit, and your ass slides down toward the front edge of the seat, your skirt now riding up far enough for me to see you aren't wearing any panties, as usual…one of my favorite things about you. You move your hands to the inside of your knees and begin to slowly slide them up your inner thighs, taunting and teasing me. The sun warming you, the wind through your hair and your gentle touch against your own flesh begins to excite you and your hands linger high up on your thighs, your thumbs on each side of your beautiful pink pussy, which is now perfectly exposed. I can see the glisten of moisture on your lips and from the Mona Lisa smile on your face, I know that you're beginning to feel the tingle of excitement. I'm finding it harder and harder to keep my eyes on the road. Without realizing it, I notice that the speedometer is up to 85.

You move one hand over your belly and slide it up under your top and begin to massage your breast. Your other hand moves over your sex and I watch as your fingers begin to move slowly over your clit, teasing it with your fingertips. You pull your top up over your bare breasts and I smile when I see that your nipples are hard and protruding.

You begin to pinch your nipples between your thumb and forefinger while the fingers of your other hand continue to play at your clit, circling and circling, moving a little faster, your head now back and your eyes closed. As we speed past the semis on the road, truckers look down at you and several give a honk. But you don't seem to notice as your fingers move faster against your clit. I reach down and rub my cock through my pants, which is now rock hard.

Your back is starting to arch from the pleasure your fingers are giving. I watch as you slide a finger inside you and begin to move it in and out. You slide it deep inside you, exploring every inch of your pussy, moving your finger in circles inside you, the ridge at the base of your fingers pressed tightly to your clit and grinding against it. Over the sound of the rushing wind, I can hear your moans and my cock grows harder, my hand moving faster on it. The car is now doing 90, but I'm completely unaware, enthralled by your sexy feet on the dash, your toes curling with pleasure, your finger, now two fingers, pumping in and out of your pussy, entranced by your moans, which are becoming louder and more frequent.

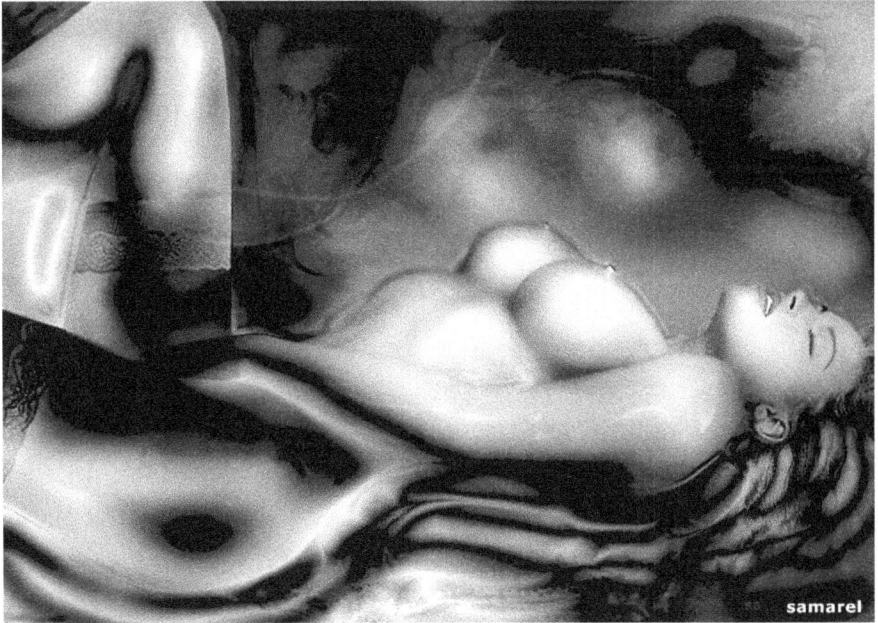

samarel

I can feel my own orgasm beginning to develop in my pants, but stop stroking my cock because I want to save it for you. You throw back your head and scream out, your back arched, your feet pressing against the dash, raising your ass off the seat, your fingers pumping in and out as your climax strikes. I watch your face, your eyes clenched tight, your mouth opened in an "O", your moans loud and deep as you cum. Your body begins to jerk in the seat and your feet kick against the dash as your pounding orgasm rocks your body.

I reach over and place my hand on your thigh as your ass settles back into the seat. You lie back, limp and sated, your feet still up on the dash. You look over at me and smile, your eyes half closed. Your expression fills my heart, but my cock is still hard and I want some of what you just had. Your hand is still covering your mound and I take it in my hand and pull it to my mouth, sucking at your fingers and licking the juices from them. I love your taste and can't stop until I get every drop of your cum from them. You lay your head back and feel the wind through your hair.

Your breasts are still exposed to the sun and I can't help but take one in my hand and knead it, loving the feel of its softness and firmness at the same time. Your nipples are still hard from your climax and I enjoy rolling them gently between my fingers. You give a soft little moan and put your hand over mine, squeezing it as it squeezes your breast. I slide my hand from under yours and you take over, both hands on your breasts, squeezing them and pulling at your nipples as my hand slides down across your belly and onto your inner thigh. You move your feet further apart on the dash, spreading your legs wider and slide your ass forward, trying to move my hand onto your sex. I understand and move the palm of my hand onto your mound and with my middle finger, I toy softly with your clit. Your eyes close and your smile grows wider as the tickle of my finger awakens your senses again. My finger moves around and over your clit, gently, slowly. You are so wet and your clit, completely swollen. My finger moves over it so smoothly, lubricated by the juices you just spilled.

My arm lies against your chest and I can feel your breathing growing heavier as I work your clit. With my palm pressing down against your mound, I slide my finger inside you and your hips rise up off the seat to take me all the way in. I start pumping you with my finger, your hips rising and falling in rhythm with my plunging finger. With my palm at the top of your mound, I move my finger deep inside you, then all the way back out with the tip pressing down against your clit. I rub the entire length of my finger across your clit with each stroke I take. As your hips rock faster, I bury a second finger deep inside you and grind my palm against your button. I press my fingers against the top wall of your pussy and slide them from the front all the way to the back, pressing directly against your g-spot. You begin to arch your back and I know you are about to cum again. I begin pumping harder in and out of you and you begin to pull on your nipples, stretching them as far as you can and pinching them hard. I put my thumb against your clit and press firmly against it while two fingers drive into you. You press your feet so hard into the dash that you leave indents in the cushion with your heels, your toes curl up, you raise your ass high into the air, your shoulders pressed hard against the seat back and you scream out. I feel your pussy clenching my fingers tightly which only makes me pump you faster. Without realizing it, my foot presses the accelerator with the same intensity my fingers are banging you and we top 100. We fly down the road, my fingers slamming into you, your pussy convulsing around them and your screams drowned out by the roar of the wind as it whips past us. Your hips and lower back begin to jerk and spasm as the waves continue to crash over you. You collapse back onto the seat and grab my hand and shout out, "Please stop! Please stop!", no longer able to stand the intensity. You lie there panting for a moment before laughing out loud and shouting "OH GOD!"

Again, I taste your juices, only this time it is from my own fingers. I look over at you and you are watching me, licking your lips with a look of hunger. I offer my fingers to you and you take them in your mouth, sucking at them greedily. You tell me "I want something more substantial" and you place your hand on the rise in my pants and rub your hand back and forth on my cock. You lean over and with both hands, undo my pants. I lift my ass off the seat and you pull them down around my knees, releasing my cock that has been straining against them for what seems like hours. It stands tall and hard and you take it in your hand and begin to stroke it gently up and down, toying with the head, toying with the shaft, toying with my balls. Your hand feels so good on me. But it makes me so happy when you slide closer to me and bend over and put your head in my lap. With your hand still wrapped around and stroking my cock, you begin to lick its head and then take it into your mouth.

www.samarelart.com

Your mouth is so wet and so warm, I feel like exploding almost instantly. You can sense my over-excitement and stop stroking me, just teasing me now with your tongue on my shaft, your hand cupping my balls, your tongue sliding over the head. Suddenly, you take me totally by surprise by sliding your mouth over my cock and plunging it all the way into your throat. I gasp and grab the back of your head. You start pumping your head up and down on my cock, your hand massaging my balls. I discover my feet are pressing against the floorboard and my ass is moving up and down on the seat, plunging my cock into your mouth. As the needle pushes past 110, I have to force myself to relax and back off. But you do not relax and continue to fuck me hard with your mouth, making me insane with desire. I can feel my orgasm building in the pit of my stomach and know I will explode into your throat in just another stroke or two.

You must be able to feel the tightening in my balls and the thickening of my cock as I prepared to explode, because you pull your mouth from me, look up and say, "That's not how I want your cum." You lie across my lap and reach down beside the seat and press the button to move the seat all the way back. You climb over the console and throw a leg over me, forcing me to lean to the side to see around you. You straddle me, leaning also to allow me to see the road, you reach down and take my engorged member into your hand. You shift over me, place the head of my cock against your slit and lower yourself down onto me. You are so wet from cumming twice already that I slide easily inside you. You put your head over my shoulder, wrap your arms around my neck and begin to move up and down on my raging cock.

The velvety wetness of your tight pussy feels incredible as you raise and lower yourself, my cock impaling you. Your sex is gripping me so tightly, there is no way I can last. You begin to move up and down faster and faster, your arms holding me around my neck, your face buried into the side of my neck. My cock is pounding in and out of you, my feet pressing hard against the floor, driving my ass up and down, trying to push deeper inside you. I can feel your swollen clit against the shaft of my cock with each hard stroke. The needle moves past 110, the wind whipping your hair around our faces, our moans becoming louder and louder. We are fucking each other so hard, so fast, so violently. You are literally bouncing on my cock and it is slamming in and out of you...115. I wrap one arm around your back, trying to steer with the other, and pull you as close as I can pull you, your tits against my chest, my ass bouncing on the seat, your ass bouncing on my cock. I feel your pussy clench me tighter and your chin is burrowing into my shoulder, your arms squeezing me around the neck.

Pressing my feet to the floor, I raise my ass off the seat, lifting you high into the air and shove my cock into you deeper than it has ever been...120. You buck wildly on top of me, forcing my cock even harder in and out of you. The wind is howling around us now, the landscape going by in a blur and as waves of ecstasy overtake us, I can't tell whose screams are whose. My cock explodes into you just as your pussy begins to spasm around me and we cum hard together. Your juices, mixed with mine, wash down my cock onto my balls. You pump me furiously, your convulsing pussy squeezing every drop of cum from me, your screams drowning out the wind as your climax racks every part of your body. As my orgasm begins to subside I look down and see the needle has topped 130. I lift my foot from the accelerator just as you collapse onto my shoulder, completely spent, your whole body shaking from the intensity of your screaming orgasm.

Only two more hours to go and we'll be there. What shall we do next?

I'll never drive the 15 without a hard-on again!

TWO FIRES – THE CLIMAX

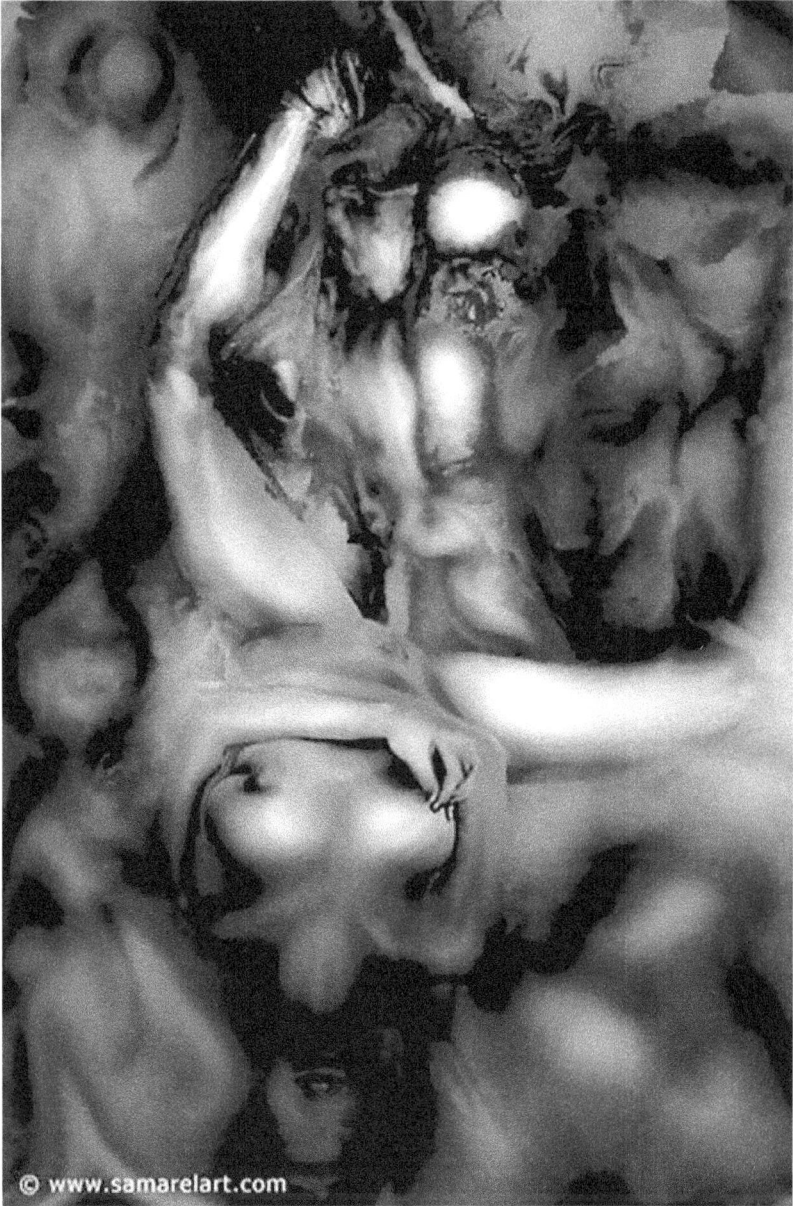

© www.samarelart.com

...We lie there together, your breasts pressed to my chest, your lips pressed to mine, the warmth of your pussy comforting around my fading member. And when the final swelling of my cock diminishes and I fall from you, I can't help but feel a longing for more.

With you in my arms, I roll over, taking you with me until I am back on top of you. I kiss down your body, savoring every inch of your flesh until I'm between your legs once again. I kiss your thighs gently, making love to them with my lips and my tongue, softly and slowly. Blowing softly against your clit again, I attempt to cool off your steaming pussy. Your eyes are closed as if in sleep, but as the cool breeze blows over your engorged clit, a faint smile begins to cross your lips. I watch your face, enraptured by how astonishingly beautiful you are, amazed that anyone so perfect, so angelic, so breathtaking, could ever be here with me. You overwhelm me and fill my heart and I find myself with my face buried in your thigh, hugging it almost desperately. I see you smiling down at me and I know that you can see what was just going through my mind.

My lips return to your thighs and I kiss them softly. I kiss your pussy gently, my lips barely touching and I watch your face as again, you smile down at me. I press my lips lightly against you and hold them there, breathing in the heavenly scent of your sex, feeling your wetness against my face, reveling in your beautiful pussy. My tongue ventures out and softly licks the folds of skin on each side of your perfect slit. They are still thick, swollen from the intensity of our lovemaking, and my soft tongue gently soothes them. I place the tip of my tongue on the sensitive skin between pussy and your brown button and starting there, I slide it slowly and softly upwards, over your opening, parting your lips gently as I go and sliding slowly and tenderly over your clit to the top of your pussy. You mutter, "mmmmm...that feels nice" and I follow the same path back down, ever so slowly, ever so gently. The tip of my tongue travels up and down your slit, barely touching you, not intending to excite, not yet anyway, only intending to soothe.

© Paul Himmel

I spend several long minutes massaging your pussy softly with my tongue and you respond, your hands moving to my head and caressing me, your fingers running through my hair. Your sounds are not ones of passion, but of contented pleasure as you moan softly. I can feel your body responding to my tongue, your bottom slowly moving up and down against my touch. I slide my hands up over your belly and tenderly rub circles with my palms, moving slowly up to your breasts and continuing the circles against your nipples. Your clit begins to swell against my tongue and I can feel your dampness against my chin and I know that your contentment with my touch will soon become excitement and need. I long to take you there and begin to move my tongue against you a little faster with slight pressure against your clit. You respond as I had hoped, your hips increasing their movement with the movement of my tongue. I lick you slowly and firmly, up and down the entire length of your pussy, gradually gaining speed, gradually applying more pressure. You say, "I'm almost ready for you...don't stop yet". My tongue continues to massage your clit and I move the tip of one finger to your opening and circle it gently. The tone of your moans is changing and I can hear that your pleasure is slowly being replaced by passion.

I work your clit a little faster, a little harder and you respond accordingly, moving your ass up and down a little faster, a little harder. With your hands at the back of my head, you pull me in tighter against your pussy. I slide my finger inside you and can feel you, so wet, so hot, so ready for me. You rock harder against my tongue and I slide a second finger into you, pressing against the walls of your pussy and sliding them slowly in and out. You moan out, "I'm ready...I want your cock...fuck me now..."

I begin to work my way up your body with my tongue. You are rocking hard against my fingers and pant "I'm gonna cum...I'm gonna cum". I slow my fingers, just enough to keep you panting but not cumming. I reach your breasts and suck greedily at your nipples before continuing up to your mouth. We kiss deeply and you suck my tongue into your mouth. You reach down and take hold of my throbbing cock and begin to stroke it. I pull my fingers from you and you place the head of my cock against your clit and rub it frantically, soaking me in your juices. You moan loudly and raise your hips up to meet me. I whisper in your ear, "Put me inside you" and you guide the head of my cock to your slit.

As my weight comes down on you, my cock inches inside your tight pussy and you rise up off the couch to drive me all the way in. You moan loudly, "fuck me... fuck me...now...make me cum..." Always eager to please, I fuck you, feeling every inch of your pussy gripping me tightly. You are so wet and I am so hard...you feel so incredible. I move in and out of your amazing, wonderful pussy, trying my best to make this sensation last but knowing that I will never be able to hold back against you clenching around my cock. Your hands grab my ass and you pull me hard into you. You are rocking hard and fast against me, forcing my cock to move faster and faster inside you. I reach underneath you with both hands and grab your ass and lift it up off the couch. My cock is deeper inside you than any cock has ever been and I pound it into you, over and over. Our bodies glisten with sweat from the heat of the fire and the heat of our frantic fucking. With my hands gripping your ass tightly, I pull your cheeks apart and begin to finger your asshole with the tip of my finger. The base of my cock rubs against your clit as I plunge deep inside you. The familiar growl starts in your throat, ever growing, and I fuck you furiously. I'm fucking you so hard, so recklessly, we are literally bouncing on the couch. Your climax builds and you rear up and buck wildly, forcing my cock ever deeper into you. You are pulling hard on my ass, digging your nails into me as I hammer my cock into you. The growl turns into a scream and bursts from your lips as the first wave of orgasm smashes into you. Your entire body screams out in ecstasy as you cum and cum over my cock, still pounding you unmercifully. You thrash violently beneath me, my cock rocking you to your core. I feel your pussy convulsing, squeezing, spasming around my throbbing member as you cum so strongly you lose all control of your body and begin to twitch fiercely under me. My cock is slamming you brutally and you are completely swallowed up by your climax, screaming uncontrollably, rocking violently, taking my cock into you to the very depths of your soul. I take my hands from your ass and lock my elbows behind your knees, forcing your legs back and your ass high into the air. My cock is stretching your pussy to its limits, pounding relentlessly. You erupt in another violent explosion of orgasm, your legs kicking out, your ass bouncing hard, your pussy gripping me tighter than I have ever been gripped, your entire body spasming beneath me, your nails ripping furrows in my back. Your face is contorted with intense ecstasy as you cum. I have never been fucked so hard and so well. I cannot hold back any longer and I gather one final burst of speed, slamming into you. I scream out and my entire body shudders as I explode inside you, my hot cum pumping into you unceasingly. Erotic pleasure washes over me and your pussy squeezes the greatest joy I have ever known from my cock. After long seconds of ecstasy, I collapse on top of you, both of our chests heaving, trying to catch our breath.

With great effort, I slide off of you and you turn onto your side to make room for me next to you on the couch. We lie together in each other's arms, our bodies trembling, your perfect breasts against my chest, our legs entwined, our faces only inches apart. You reach up and touch my cheek and you smile at me. The last embers of the fire glow softly in the fireplace just as the fire of our spent passion glows on our faces. And then, just as I've always fantasized, you say those three little words that every woman says after having incredible, mind-blowing sex...

"I gotta pee"

To which there is only one response...

"Grab me a beer on the way back, would ya?"

DEAR FANTASY GIRL...

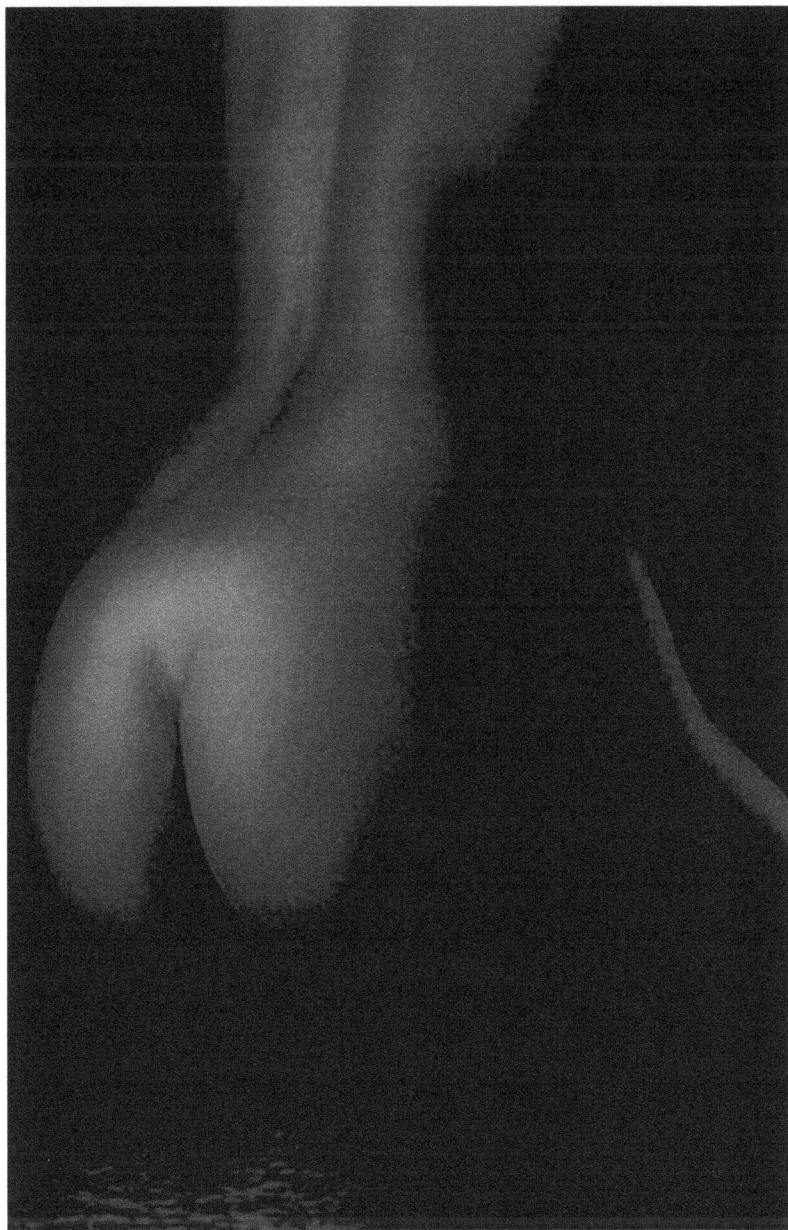

It's 4:00 in the morning and I can't sleep with thoughts of you running through my mind. I miss you so much. I close my eyes and I see you before me, beautiful and radiant. I open them and I see you in the shadows, the silhouette of your inviting body against the wall, just out of my reach. I stretch my hand out toward you and you reach out for me, but our fingers cannot quite touch. I ache to hold you. If I could only pull you into my arms, I would never let you go again. I need the taste of your lips. I need to caress and feel the caress of your wonderful touch. How I wish that I could feel your naked skin against mine, not making love, just reveling in the warmth of your flesh transmitting heat to every inch of my being. That is when I feel closest to you, yet it is only in fantasy. I long for the day when you will lie naked before me and allow me to run my hands over every inch of you, leaving no area unexposed to the warmth of my touch. And at that moment when warmth turns to heat, and heat into fire, it is then that I will enter you. And when passion turns to ecstasy, at that moment of perfect union, it will be so much more than just my seed that I leave inside you.

I have become so smitten by you that even the air I breathe carries your aroma. And with each exhale, I breathe out more of my heart to you. If I do not stop breathing, soon you will have all of my heart.

Why aren't you here?

Photo credits

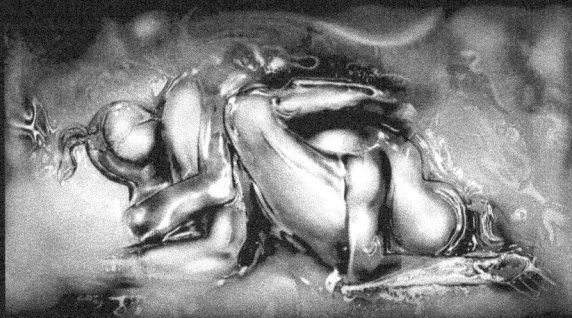

Burst of energy

A burst of energy that is the best way to describe the work and website of Samarel. It's so full of lust, desire and life it's hard to get it in words.

If you imagine that sexual lust is a bouncing streaming energy that goes trough your body and brings you the ecstasy feel your after. Well Samarel is capable of visualizing this in his work. Bright, hard, liquid flushes of color integrating with the human body, making the body alive. Vibrating between lovers, feasting on each other's energy.

I think it's done in a great way. Using the images manipulator toolboxes are hardly giving us masterpieces. But sometimes there are artists that are going beyond the easy effect they provide. They are used to visualize the artists ideas and to complement what pure photography can bring us. Have fun feasting on the images of Samarel and be sure to visit the website. It is definitely worth spending some time over there.

(The Art of Love)

www.samarelart.com

Additional photo credits

Untitled page 15 © Bjorn Oldsen

LasVegasview page 39 © Steve Anderson Photography

Christinewinery page 42 © Steve Anderson Photography

Elevator page 48 © Martin Toye

Aliciatahitiinn page 59 © Steve Anderson Photography

Tracing Your Smile page 61 © Martin Toye

Hold Me and Kiss Me page 72 © Martin Toye

Touchy Hands page 94 © Martin Toye

Watching You page 103 © Martin Toye

A Hug page 121 © Martin Toye

A Nap I... page 146 © Martin Toye

Sasha page 147 © Steve Anderson Photography

Untitled page 151 © Jean-Paul Four

Untitled page 153 © Jean-Paul Four

Shoe Fetish page 160 © Jean-Paul Four

StudioBar page 179 © Steve Anderson Photography

Siesta Next to the Highway page 191 © Martin Toye

Untitled page 206 © Paul Himmel

A Nap II... page 210 © Martin Toye

Galleries and Websites

Samarel

www.samarelart.com

Martin Toye

www.adesnudarte.com.ar/v2

Steve Anderson

www.MyFineArtNudes.com

Commercial work:

www.SteveAndersonPhotography.com

Jean-Paul Four

www.jpfgallery.com

Bjorn Oldsen

www.oldsen.de

Paul Himmel

www.paul-himmel.de

Naked Noises   www.nakednoises.com

Art of Love   www.lovechess.nl/artoflove

Acknowledgements

My very special thanks to Laura Monica Cucu for her invaluable expertise and dedication to this project. Laura handled every aspect of the publication of this collection, and I do mean every. Thank you for your patience, your guidance and your diligence. It never would have been published without you.

To Sandra Mato for my introduction to blogging, for her constant encouragement, and when encouragement stopped working, for pushing me to stop procrastinating. I would still be editing the first blog, if not for her.

To Margie Benton for hosting my first blog and giving me my first public exposure, for convincing me that I could be successful in this genre, for teaching me how to properly code a blog, for creating incredible banners for me and so many other things. Without her, there would never have been a Night Xposed blog.

To all of my loyal readers on Myspace who supported the Night Xposed blog, made it a lot of fun and consistently took it to the top. I love you guys!

And last, but very far from least, to Katelyn. It's all your fault.